Thorns
on the
Rose

Sheron Chambers Jefferson

Trilogy Christian Publishers
A Wholly Owned Subsidary of Trinity Broadcasting Network
2442 Michelle Drive
Tustin, CA 92780

For information, address Trilogy Christian Publishing
Rights Department, 2442 Michelle Drive, Tustin, Ca 92780.
Trilogy Christian Publishing/ TBN and colophon are trademarks of Trinity Broadcasting Network.

For information about special discounts for bulk purchases, please contact Trilogy Christian Publishing.

Manufactured in the United States of America

10 9 8 7 6 5 4 3 2 1

Library of Congress Cataloging-in-Publication Data is available.

ISBN 978-1-64773-764-1 (Print Book)
ISBN 978-1-64773-765-8 (ebook)

Transformed by the Experiential
Knowledge of the Lord Jesus Christ

With a New Perspective Came a New Life

Therefore, since Christ suffered for us in His body, arm yourselves also with the same mind (attitude/perspective), because he who has suffered in the flesh has ceased from sin. As a result, they no longer live the rest of their lives in the flesh for evil human desires, but rather for the Will of God. For you have spent enough of our past lifetime doing what pagans choose to do—walking in debauchery, lust, lewdness, drunkenness, orgies, carousing, revelries, and abominable idolatry. (1 Pet. 4:1–3 NIV)

Though He was a Son, yet He learned obedience by the things which He suffered. (Heb. 5:8)

If we are children, then we are heirs—heirs of GOD and co-heirs with Christ, if indeed we share in His sufferings that we may also shear in His Glory. For I consider the sufferings of this present time are not worthy to be compared with the Glory which shall be revealed in us. (Rom. 8:17–18)

Contents

Acknowledgments

Giving honor to the Holy, Sovereign Lord God Almighty, my everything. Through Your gift of Salvation and new birth, because of Your Presence living in me, I can face victoriously whatever comes. You are my source. You are my God, and I am Your child.

To my children, who are my greatest treasures and motivation—Waymond, Robert, Shawn, Shannon, Stephen, Darwin, and Daylin, and their children to come. Writing this book, I hope to leave a legacy of encouraging faith and obedience in the Lord while nurturing an intimate relationship as their life's priority. That they would live as if they believe God's promises of His presence in them, with them, and for them according to His Word, as they have been taught and have experienced. I hope to give a clear understanding of who I am and why. I pray that any of and all the hurt I have caused be reversible. That they will forgive me. Live a life of honor, trusting God's Word as priority all the days of their lives. That they would rest in trusting, that God will turn trials and tribulations into heavenly treasures, dark into light, and death into life. I share my testimony so when life is hard and everything seems to be going against you, when you are making continuous bad choices, know that God is good. He loves you and has a plan for your life for good and not to harm you, but you must wholeheartedly surrender it all to Him. In my experience, God will use all the horrible mess His child makes as an opportunity to show Himself mighty and bless you. Reminding you of when you were at the place of surrender so that you will trust, turn from, and give Him your life and be blessed.

To my mama also, who prayed for me through thick and thin throughout my many years of prideful rebellion. I appreciate her as my number one cheerleader; she loved me much and made me feel special when I thought I was not good enough and felt most inadequate. I am thankful for all that she taught me, the what-to-do and the what-not-to-do. Her sacrifices and examples, I am so grateful for, for her beautiful example of a woman, a mother, and for her undying influence in my life.

I am grateful to have been blessed with my amazing sister, who's always been there for me. Thank you, Renee, the best sister in the world, from the depth of my heart, for always being on my side. Renee has been for me what Aaron was to Moses, encouraging and supporting me to answer the call of God in my life, bringing her gifts where I lacked. She has supported me since I came into the world in every way, encouraged and pushed me to my potential, waiting for me to see my anointing. She would not and did not allow me to give up or quit.

I want to give a special thanks to my niece Tracy, who is like a little sister to me. Tracy has shown me selfless, enduring love and generosity, always there in my time of need.

I want to say a special appreciation to Pastor Willie Dalgity of Set Free Yucaipa Ministries.

There are many more that have been encouraging witnesses to my transformation. Thank you. You know who you are!

Preface

Writing this book, telling my testimony, has been a form of healing that has bought me freedom, vulnerability to share all that I have come to understand about being a child of God, being broken and then transformed, and becoming who and doing what God purposed for my life. The more difficult the trial, the more my faith grew. I grew closer and closer to my Lord.

I have heard it said and believe in an old proverb, "A child's character or behavior will resemble that of his father or mother." Children eventually come to reflect the attitude and behaviors of his or her parents, saying simply children act and behave in the same way they see their parents. Children look like and learn from their parents' characteristics, both good and bad. I am also a strong believer that the fruit does not fall far from the tree; all children have some characteristics from their parents, and therefore, grandparents as well. We pick up things from our parents that they did and did not do, acting out their true values and beliefs, not what they said they valued and believed. That is learned behavior. I was not aware of the strong influence my mother and father had on me until I became an adult. That was a large part of my problem; I call them thorns. Without conscious awareness, I was a mixture of the two of them, the good and bad. I had inherited what I now consider ungodly spirits or soul ties. For example: adultery, fear, feeling inadequate, being materialistic, self-centeredness, not valuing the ways of God regarding relationships and people, divorce, substance abuse, and several others stemming from false beliefs and thinking errors. Also, I have five children. I hope this will help them overcome. They lost their fathers at very young ages, under one year and no more than four years old, yet somehow they have demonstrated several ways of their father that they were too young to have seen.

Recognizing my need for change started with my process of seeking treatment for drug addiction. Starting with a rehabilitation program focusing on the twelve steps, then adding Gods Word, learning and believing, choosing to obey the Bible, attending church, it all changed my lifestyle. During the process, I understood and believed more about Jesus Christ and received Him as my Savior first. It was eight years later, after confessing Jesus Christ as Savior, while living a defeated, powerless, godless life, that I surrendered wholeheartedly to Jesus as my Lord, Redeemer, and Healer. I conducted myself believing God's Word as the truth. I obeyed more and more, better and better, and closer and closer I drew to Him and experienced an intimate relationship with Him. The first change for me was a promise, a rule to myself; whatever the Bible, God's Word, said, that was what I would do, to the best of my understanding. I was being transformed. I began to perceive things differently now and getting to know the ways of Christ. I gained awareness of my false beliefs, their consequences, and my carnal, twisted mind. I prayed for healing and deliverance from my ungodly ways, and my prayers were answered, in the name of Jesus.

I believe it is God's will to stop and break generational curses and strongholds. It is my responsibility as a steward and the parent of the children God had given to me, a born-again disciple of Christ Jesus, to live set free, a slave to righteousness according to the Word, as an example to teach my children, grandchildren, and others the way to Jesus Christ. To live pleasing the Lord God and not turn away from Him and back to ungodliness, hard-heartedness, and idol worship. Therefore, I give you my testimony with hope in the Lord that you will live free indeed and continue to grow in the grace and knowledge of Christ Jesus, the Lord and Savior (2 Pet. 3:18).

Matthew 12:43–45 says, "When an impure spirit comes out of a person it goes through arid places seeking rest and does not find it. Then it says, 'I will return to the house I left.' When it arrives, it finds the house unoccupied, swept clean and put in order. Then it goes and takes with it seven other spirits more wicked than itself, and they go in and live there. The final condition of that person is worse than the first." That is how it will be with this wicked generation. I pray I have taught my children to live a close relationship, trusting in the Lord. The house is clean; rebellion, idolatry, drunkenness, lust, sexual immorality are gone. The house is clean and in order. Now you must continue and keep it clean so that the impure spirits your parents were delivered from, which have been removed, cannot return. Moreover, you now can follow the example set before you to live your life set apart to the Lord and teach this to your children as an inheritance. I am putting my faith to work; I pray that the Lord bless my efforts to tell my testimony. I have been completely truthful and honest. I did not know how to tell it and protect everybody's feelings based on their perspective, and for that, I apologize. Please forgive me. I did not intend to hurt or harm anyone, only to give insight and encouragement from my perspective for others that find themselves, as I was, a slave to sin, wounded, and blind, in need of healing and deliverance from ungodly hurts, habits, and hang-ups.

Introduction

Thorns on the Rose is my story of how the Lord God broke me down to build me up and transformed me, presented in an analogy or like a parable. Simply said, my story is how God took me, one of the most self-centered, selfish individuals on the planet, and loved me in to a selfless servant for Christ and changed my entire life. God changed the way I think and perceive life, giving me a new way to respond. Using an analogy is a comparison between two things, for the purpose of explanation or clarification. A parable is an earthly story with a heavenly meaning. Something on earth is compared to something in heaven so that the heavenly truth can be understood better in light of the earthly illustration. Jesus taught using parables and was known as the master of the parables. He used parables to make abstract ideas concrete. It is better to see a picture than to attempt to visualize a thing. What I like about parables is that it forces people to think for themselves and to discover the truth for themselves. That is my hope, that the reader make a connection comparing the here-and-now earth with heaven, something happening on earth to guide the thoughts of people heavenward. I think of *Thorns on the Rose* like a parable, an earthly story with a heavenly meaning. Something on earth is compared to something in heaven so that the heavenly truth can be understood better in light of earthly illustration. My gratefulness is to the Lord Jesus for His profound truths revealed to me through His Presence in my life. Like the rose, I find myself intrigued that God has created many varieties of people differing in appearance, purpose, abilities, strengths, weaknesses, struggles, and needs. God beautifully created us all in His image. He intentionally, single-handedly knows what it will take to get us to our full purpose. He provides those needs. Thorns are defining moments, trials, events, circumstances, and situations that are life-changing.

Second Corinthians 4:17 describes *thorns* as our light and momentary troubles, afflictions.

In John 19:1–4, 30, and 20, it tells us of an example of thorns and roses as Jesus suffered affliction and sorrow, trading death for life.

Hebrews 5:8 tells us that though He was the Son, He learned obedience from the things He suffered. One may perceive a thorn as some kind of drudgery, irritation, fear, or temporary condition. A thorn on the rose is a hard surface that pricks and sticks, deterring one to protect the rose. Thorns get your attention and cause you to examine what you are doing.

Looking at 2 Corinthians 12:7–10, there is an example of the benefits thorns produce in order to keep us from becoming conceited and trust that God's grace is sufficient and more than enough for you, for when I am weak, then I am strong. Showing us how difficult roads often lead to beautiful destinations, like the cross for Jesus preceded the crown.

In my experience of the Presence of the Holy Spirit, I received this new perception and changed thinking, which brought about a new way of life. This is where the title of this book comes from. It has taken me many years while still battling negative character to write this book. No more excuses. This is it. I have used every excuse possible you may be familiar with, such as that no one is interested in what I may have to say, that I am a nobody, then the fear of failing, fear that people might think I'm trying to be something I am not, people not believing that it was the Holy Spirit who told me to write this. Feelings of inadequacy, fear, pride, laziness, and doubt—to sum it up, my strongholds. None of that matters because I know that I must write the story. God told me to, and this is all that matters. I won't let the enemy rob me. Now, let me show you the correlation as I see it in a healthy rose's process of growth and a healthy child of God's growth toward spiritual maturity.

Have you ever considered that most people love roses but hate the thorns? Unfortunately, you cannot have an authentic rose that does not have thorns; they are a part of the same beautiful creation. Roses are symbolic of love and beauty. For a rose to mature into its full potential, it is important to match the right variety with the right region and take measures that will help the rose thrive, enduring season after season. There are different methods in the preparation for planting the more than thirteen thousand varieties with many characteristics that you find appealing, like the shape, size, color, and purpose. Note the similarities in describing the child of God and the rose.

There is a hybrid (tea rose), beautifully shaped and colorful, purposely used for appearances.

The floribunda is the most colorful of all, and each bush has many blossoms rather than having just one to a stem.

The grand flora is a cross between the two previous mentioned roses that grows to be quite tall, with several rose clusters to a stem.

The climber is the rose that you can train to stretch vine-like along fences and walls.

The miniature is intricate and tiny, perfect for planting in a container. As shrub and landscape, they are put to use, being quite hardy and resistant to pest and diseases. They come in many shapes and sizes.

Tree roses get their name from being grafted to a long stem, giving them the appearance of a tree. They require a bit more care than the other types.

For the best outcome, roses are planted in early spring, giving them time to take root before sprouting several weeks later, in the warmer winter weather. Pruning or shearing keeps the roses healthy, promoting the growth of blooms and keeping them in a perfect shape. Working with roses, applying wisdom, protects us from the sting of thorns on the rose. Fertilize them to feed a few times in the season. Mulching the rose bed helps keep pest away and distribute more nutrients to the rose.

To plant a rose, we must dig a hole, decide on the spot with good sunlight, not crowded out with other roots or branches. The rose must have loose soil with drainage so that the roots have room to grow. The rose must be frequently watered thoroughly and fertilized a few times a season to stabilize the plant. Mulching the area that the rose is in keeps the temperature consistent during the early stages of growth. The rose must be pruned to keep them beautiful and healthy and prevent rotting and disease. This encourages new blooms to grow. The key is to prune with a goal toward opening the bushes' growth.

I have always loved roses and what they represent, the symbol of balance, the expression of beauty, promise, hope, new beginnings, joy, protection, and mature love. In contrast, the thorn symbolizes defense, loss, and thoughtlessness.

Therefore, from my newly gained perception, I have learned the values of these in many different events, situations, and circumstances that have occurred in my life that I call thorns. I have gained enhanced appreciation for their divine purposes. In my development and the beauty of the Lord's work, when I reflect back over my life, there have been many thorns used to bring about my transformation to create a better rose. The beauty of the rose is seen in correlation with being victorious conquerors, no longer slaves to sin or the temptations of the world, and personally identifying with the death and resurrection of Christ Jesus, the Lord. The definition of the root word *victory* is "final and complete supremacy or superiority in battle or war, success in the contest or struggling involving the defeat of an opponent or the overcoming of obstacles." Praise the Lord!

First Corinthians 15:7 confirms that we are conquerors, which means to get the better of any completion, competitor, or struggle; to master, suppress, prevail over, overwhelm, surmount over; to gain superiority; to subdue; to vanquish; to crush; and to defeat. Praise God!

As you read *Thorns on the Rose*, a story about me and my life being broken down, overcoming, and transforming, you will read that it was not easy, but God was there with His plan. The reward for this journey thus far and on into eternity is unfathomable, beautiful, and fulfilling, beyond anything I could have imagined. Receiving salvation through Christ Jesus is more than a guaranteed ticket to heaven when you die, as I once thought. Salvation has shown me that I have choices to get the best of life here on earth now. I am grateful to the Lord God for His power to overcome the ungodly thinking patterns I had developed and walked with many years habitually. I am His child and the righteousness of Christ. He is my God, my Father, and He loves me. I am no longer hopeless, helpless, and defeated. I am free, no longer bound. I have surrendered to the One who has conquered the world and death. Christ, the Lord God's only begotten Son. My story, *Thorns on the Rose*, is about being transformed—meaning a thorough, dramatic change in form or appearance, a metamorphosis during the life cycle.

> "But the one whom God raised from the dead did not see decay. Therefore, my friends, I want you to know that through Jesus the forgiveness of sins is proclaimed to you. Through Him everyone who believes is Set Free from every sin, a justification you were not able to obtain without Jesus under the law of Moses" (Acts 13:37–39).

Roman 12:2 confirms it takes a lot of choices, consistency, and willingness to let go of old ways and allow yourself to let God teach you to think in a new way regarding old and familiar information. By no means is this easy apart from the Holy Spirit, but by the power of God and His indwelling Holy Spirit, all things are possible.

Thorns on the Rose is a metaphor of my life, when I thought within my old nature, what God calls bad, I saw as good, as a carnal-minded man of flesh, representing the enemy to God, loving the things of the world, destructive, harmful, self-centered, unloving, and ungodly.

The thorns that symbolized hurt, pain, difficult life situations, and blockers that came between me and what I thought was good and I wanted. People, places, and things my sinful nature valued rather than the Lord's perfect will.

God's way is the beauty of the rose. The rose symbolizes the beauty of how the power of God carries out His plan in the Spirit through His love, mercy, and grace by faith to bring what is His back to His light from the darkness. The rose represents beauty, perfection, purity, wholeness, healthiness, godliness, and selflessness. *Beauty* is defined as "pleasing to the senses or mind aesthetically; perfection of form, color, etc.; noble and spiritual qualities: of very high standards, excellence: stateliness or pleasing proportion." Beauty is pure, free from anything inferior or contaminating, flawless and undiluted.

This book tells of my life without Christ and then the process of being transformed after surrendering my life to Him as Savior and then as Lord. After trial upon trial, hit after hit, I kept fighting against the Lord's ways. He knew how to break me down. I was not able to fight against Him and how far He was willing to go to get what was His.

> "Just as He chose us in Him before the foundation of the world, that we would be Holy and blameless before Him" (Eph. 1:4).

> "'For I know the plans I have for you,' declares the Lord, 'plans to prosper you and not to harm you, plans to give you Hope and a future'" (Jer. 29:11).

"And you also were included in Christ when you heard The Word of Truth, The Gospel of your Salvation. Having believed, you were marked in Him with a seal, the promised Holy Spirit, who is a deposit guaranteeing our inheritance until the redemption of those who are God's possession—to the Praise of His Glory" (Eph. 1:13–14). I was a wounded, hard-hearted, hardheaded believer in Jesus, learning to let go of my old man and grow into the grace and knowledge of the Lord Jesus Christ and His finished work of the cross. The Lord's Presence brought hope and change, with the evidence and joy of seeing God's hand on my life. My testimony of transformation shared to encourage others to seek the Lord, allow Him to set you free, give you a new mind to grow in faith and obedience, to see differently according to the Word of Truth and live accordingly.

Second Corinthians 12:7–10 speaks of Paul's thorn in the flesh. I use this as an example of how God used my many sinful strongholds to increase my reliance on His Grace and Power; like freedom, hope is also a child of Grace, and God's grace cannot be stopped. Hope can sometimes be an elusive thing, and occasionally it must come to us with pain, like thorns on the rose. One thing you must remember while reading my story is that it is my personal confession. I was God's most retarded daughter, which means I learned slower than others did. God knows me as the kind of child that would not just obey but had to get the whooping before I learned to obey. There are different varieties of God's Children; some are compliant, and others strong-willed, as well as those in between. All of God's children will get what and where God's planned for them; it's just that some of us, because of our strong will, will be more beat-up and scared when we get there.

This book tells of my testimony in the form of a metaphor and the significance of the thorns on the rose. My story of a changed perception that taught me to fully appreciate and honor thorns, trusting their divine purpose while recognizing the beauty of the thorns as a significant part of the rose as a whole. My trials, tribulations, and iniquities are disguised blessings and opportunities that God allowed for strength of faith to grow me in the Grace and Knowledge of the Lord Jesus Christ. You will hear my perception of how passing tests today is a testimony of overcoming temptations for tomorrow. How I received this spiritual perception and value of the process and the time of nurturing and care the Lord is giving to bring me to perfection. How God took and transformed me through thorns so that I would bear beauty like the rose. He positioned me, took my ugly, and gave His Beauty, my weakness for His Strength. The thorns on the rose are seen in John 15:1–17. Here it explains the vine and the branches as an excellent picture of our relationship and dependence to God in life. That we must choose to be connected to the Vine, to also surrender to Him as Lord, be trimmed, cut back, cleaned, and reduced to nothing but His Grace, Mercy, Faith, and Hope. I have found that through the storms and trials of life, Jesus keeps me stable, like an anchor to a ship. By His Love, Mercy, and Grace, He adds Wisdom, Reliance, and Strength. As we remain connected by Faith and Knowledge of who He is, obeying His Word, letting perseverance do its work, we produce healthy and lasting fruit in the form of love, service, and endurance.

I hope my story will encourage others who find their lives acquainted with sorrow encouraged to hold on to the Living Word of our loving God as to an immoveable anchor in the storms of life. Jesus is able to keep you and continuously has brought me through many trials, hardships, tribulations, and afflictions. He has shaped my perspective as to what I value and believe. When God's Presence became the focal point of my consciousness, all the pieces of my life began to have purpose and fulfillment. I now have a desire and respect for Gods ways, a more intimate relationship with the Godhead, and that has produced a more beautiful and meaningful life.

The Beginning

Choosing

Rose: To best understand me, I must start with even before I was born. I come from good soil. My family has a great sense of pride for our bloodline. My mom is from Boley, Oklahoma, an all-black town, declared a National Historic Landmark by Congress on May 15, 1975. Boley, Oklahoma, was established in 1903 and incorporated in 1905 as an all-black town on Creek Nation, Indian Territory. The population quickly grew to 4,200 in 1912, when Booker T. Washington came to Boley to document its progress. My mom's father, Joseph Langston McCormick, was the sheriff of the town, while her mother, Anne Mae Crawford, was a homemaker and the Reverend of the church. My grandfather, a big tall man of Indian heritage, in 1932, as sheriff, led in the capture of the notorious bank robber Birdwell, of the Pretty Boy Floyd gang, gaining the public's attention, putting Boley on the map. My grandparents were honorable people with admirable character, strong Christian faith, values, and beliefs that cared for others and family, and although they did not have much, they had no lack and worked for everything they did have. They owned their home and property and were married until death separated them.

My mother was the third eldest child of their six children. My mother was a strikingly beautiful woman; some people have said she looked like a black Elizabeth Taylor, although her complexion was not very much different. She was extremely fair skinned, with flowing wavy hair, more than all her siblings. Mom was attending college when she chose to marry at an early age a handsome young man also from Boley that was in the military, as a way out of the country, and moved to the city of Los Angeles, California. In that union was born my four older siblings. They divorced after ten years.

Thorn: Mom believed in marriage and went back to the altar four additional times. However, she bore three more children—my sister Vaughnchetta; myself, Sheron; and my little brother, Shelly III—but was not married to our fathers. I was born in 1958, and we lived in South Central Los Angeles.

Rose: As a single mother, she was very protective of her children. She gave her all to train us with values, how we look, to be clean, obedient, respectful people that took care of one another and valued family unity while making us know we were loved. She consistently taught us to take care of what we had because things didn't come easy, and just because we didn't have much was no reason not to look clean and kept as anyone else. Although I remember when Mom, throughout all the living room furniture, said it was raggedy and she would rather sit on the floor until she was able to replace it. Our house was usually small compared to how many of us there was, and Saturday was housecleaning day. We would pull weeds from the yard and clean the front porch before playtime. Mom taught us if the porch and front yard are dirty, the house is probably dirty too. We had no car, so early Saturday mornings, Mom would load the family's dirty clothes up in our toy wagon and she would take four of us and walk seven blocks to the Laundromat. Saturday housecleaning was detailed and included serious time scrubbing walls and baseboards. Mom taught us to be detailed and focused on cleaning as well as doing the laundry and ironing. She was known for her good cooking, and she made an exceptional peach cobbler. Her pies were the best because she perfected the crust. My mother provided for us the best she could as a stay-at-home mom, homemaker with a welfare check, and the help of good and loyal friends.

Thorn: Mama had an illness and often did not feel well. She had beautiful shoulder-length wavy hair, and to make her feel better, she enjoyed when my sister or I would scratch her scalp and brush through her hair. Mama went beyond limits to give all we needed, doing all she could to show her seven children how much she loved us. To the extent of criminal behavior, writing bad checks to provide during Christmas and Easter, and for school clothes, and she almost went to jail repeated times.

My daddy number 1 was Otis Chambers (I will explain a little further in my story what daddy number 1 means). I never met his parents, although I did know his siblings and their children. His mother and father raised their family of six children as Christians with faith in Jesus Christ as Lord and Savior in the state of Texas. He was the third eldest child of six siblings. My father's parents owned their home and remained married until death separated them. My dad had looks like that of his Indian heritage, with deep-brown skin and wavy black hair. He was handsome, with a distinct chin, nose, and cheekbones and deep-set eyes of Indian heritage, with muscular limbs, wide shoulders, notable and large hardworking hands, and was tall in structure at six feet, five inches. He had been a soldier of the United States Army.

My daddy was very friendly and personable, kind, and generous, liked by all. His profession was a carpenter and painter. Monday through Friday, he worked.

Thorn: Friday through Saturday night, he drank and gambled. His personality changed—he was loud and outgoing. He had been previously married and had an adult son and daughter. Come Sunday, he was suited up and at church.

My parents met having many of the same friends and frequenting the same places. My mom waited tables at bars for extra income. With both of them being tall and attractive, they were the life of the party, with outgoing personalities, and my dad was crazy about my mom.

The world is filled with wonder when seen through the eyes of a child. My earliest memories of life are happy ones.

Thorn: I have come to understand that I was born into an unstable environment that lacked structure. My family moved almost monthly. I have five older siblings and one younger—two sisters and four brothers. Intentionally, we were raised to be very close; we slept three to a bed.

Thorn: The eldest four have the same father; the remaining three of us have different fathers. The eldest sister, Renee, then brother Samuel are a year apart. Three years younger is my second eldest brother, Langston. My third older brother, Gerald, is two years younger than Langston, and my second older sister, Vaughnchetta—we call her Vaughn—is three years younger than Gerald and fifteen months older than I am. Baby brother Shelly is six years younger than me. Langston and Vaughnchetta did not live with us. Their early years, they were allowed to live with their aunts, their father's sisters, until the age of nine. They both would come to visit our family throughout the years.

Thorn: My mama told me of when she took me to Boley at six months old, excited to show her daddy her pretty new baby. He took me in his arms and said, "Yes, Dean, she is beautiful, but listen to me, she's going to be mean." Mom said that hurt her feelings, but truer words have never been spoken—he told the truth. I was a happy, loving, affectionate child, always hugging and touching, with very outgoing personality, talkative, making up stories, and singing song.

Rose: I remember the fun we had when all the family would gather at our house for the different holidays. My first- and second-generation uncles, aunts, cousins, and close friends of the family.

Thorn: Alcohol was always also there at every celebration. Other than that, my mom did not drink. My cousins and I would sneak into the room because we were not allowed in there where the adults were "talking grown-folks business," and we would sip the drinks until we would get too silly and give ourselves away. That was my first experience with alcohol.

The Early Years

The eldest sibling, my sister Renee, is twelve years older than I, and it was she who took care of me when she was not in school. And she hated it because I was spoiled rotten and manipulative.

Thorn: My mother would make her take me with her as she played with her friends. She hated to take me to the store, where I would throw a tantrum when I did not get what I wanted. She once left me at the store, where I was lying on the ground in the midst of a tantrum when I did not get what I wanted. She left me at the store throwing a tantrum and went home to tell Mom. She told Renee she'd better go get her baby. "And give my baby whatever she wants." Life was wonderful when it was all about me. When I trace my happiest thoughts, it is when I was the baby in the family, before the birth of my brother. I have a few detailed memories of events, people, and places, only a few memories of my own with Daddy being there. My older siblings remember more of that time, and they have shared their memories with me. My earliest memories, and happiest, are before I started school, when Mom and I were home alone all day, before she had my younger brother, Shelly, and my other siblings were at school. Mom watched soap operas until the Helm's

Bakery truck came down our street with all kinds of pastries and other goodies. Mom had a running tab with them. She would take me to the truck, which would stop in the street outside of our house daily, and I could have whatever I wanted. My favorites were potato chips and cream-filled doughnuts. That was possibly the beginning of my weight problem. My daddy number 1 would come home from work, and we would exchange long, tight hugs, kisses, and smiles. He would shower and smell so good; I'll never forget the cologne he used was Old Spice. Then he would sit me on his lap, and I would pick paint drops off his face, arms, and hands.

Thorn: From my beginning, I felt different from other children, being off the chart in comparison to my age group in size, height, and weight, and I continued growing rapidly. Everywhere I went, people would question how old I was. When I started school, the teacher said, "Little girl, you must be in the wrong class," and my mother spoke up to say, "No, this is where she belongs." This happened repeatedly to me all my childhood. When speaking of me to clarify, people would say, "You mean big Sheron?" My mom always introduced me with a smile of pride on her face as her pretty little fat girl. At a very young age, I was a talker. Mama called me her Polly Parrot and said I would talk her ear off. I would often repeat what I would overhear and report it to Mama. It was then she named me Rona Barrett, a well-known television reporter at that time.

Rose: I loved to sing and make up songs, stories, and poems. I had a vibrant imagination and would create stories to tell. In addition, at playtime I enjoyed pretending to be the mother when playing house, and teacher when playing school. Also, when there were gatherings with lots of friends and family, I had what I identified as a peace rug, where if there was a conflict among us children, I would sit us down to resolve it. I believe these were the beginning evidence of the presence on my gift. A gift is something that you are instinctually born with that gives you unique skills and abilities (Eph. 2:10, Exod. 35:10, James 1:17, 1 Pet. 4:10–11). Being so big, I was very clumsy and would fall, bump into things, and knock things over often. I didn't realize it, but I'm sure it didn't help that I sucked my thumb while I carried a fuzzy blanket until the age of twelve, then six feet tall.

Thorn: Through my eyes as a child, it seemed that because my father was in the home, I received special attention and favor. While my dad was there, I was the princess. My mother and father loved me and spoiled me, made me feel special. That was the best time of my life as I remember, when it was all about me.

Thorn: Another of my deepest memories is when I came home from school in the first grade and found my family had moved out of our house. There was nothing there. I was taken across the street by my neighbors, whom I had spent lots of time with, playing at their house with their children and going to their temple. They were Jehovah's Witnesses. I stayed with them what seemed like an eternity, but in actuality, it was until that evening, when my mom came to get me. As a child, I had no understanding. All I knew was how I felt, again the feeling of rejection, sadness, fear, hurt, unsafety, and abandonment. These feelings I recognize as those that are most familiar throughout my life.

My daddy number 1 moved out of our house when I was around the age of five years old, and it seemed like my world shifted. As a child with no understanding of why he was gone, all I knew was that I felt disappointment, sadness, abandonment, rejection, and I no longer felt special. My daddy, who had made my life feel right, had left me. I thought, if he loved me, he would not have left me, so I must not be lovable. There must be something wrong with me. At around the age of nine, I started having a repeated dreadful nightmare. In this nightmare, I would be outside in the front yard. We lived in a corner house. Then a big black car with tinted windows would come speeding around the corner and throw my daddy number 1 Otis's limp, bloody body out onto the curb and speed off. I was awakened in tears by that dream for many years. It is safe to say I worried about him, being aware that he gambled, a lot, especially when he was not in communication with me. It seemed Daddy moved from state to state, so one of the most important relationships to me was reduced to phone calls, him sending money, and two to three visits a year, spending weeks together. Dad number 1 always had a nice place to live and a very nice lady friend when I'd see him, and most of them had children. When I would meet her, it seemed that Dad had informed her of how much he loved and missed me; she responded appropriately, as if she loved me too. It was during these visits that he'd take me shopping for clothes because of my continuously growing size. My clothes were very costly, shopping at Lane Bryant even as a child. I was ashamed to shop there because I didn't like identifying with the obese women that shopped there, but that was where the clothes and shoes fit me.

When I was six, my little brother, Shelly, was born. I was not happy about that; it was not about me anymore, then it was all about him because of his father, who was present now. He had the attention and favor.

Thorn: My brother's father sold drugs in the form of pills; I later learned he was big in the game. I remember thinking they were candy because of the many different colors in different containers. How I wished I could get into the locked closet where they were kept. As I got older, judging and having opinions, I resented him and lost respect for him for what he did and stood for. Matthew 7:2 tells us, "For what judgment you judge, you shall be judged: for with whatever judgment you judge, you will be judged; and with whatever measure you measure, it will be measured to you." The Word of the Lord is the Truth.

In her senior year of high school, my sister Renee gave birth to my niece Tracy, two years after my brother was born. They were like having two younger siblings because they were so close in age.

Rose: We are a very close family. My mom raised Tracy as her own while Renee finished school and went to college and worked. Growing up, I remember lots of family gatherings at our house with grandparents, great-aunts and great-uncles, aunts and uncles, and first and second cousins. From time to time, my mother's siblings lived with us and she babysat for their children on and off throughout my childhood, and that made us closer to our cousins. We did go to church as a family on occasion some Sundays, Easter, Mother's Day, and I attended summer vacation Bible school, which was a high-lighted occasion during the summer. The song "How Great Thou Art" would bring me to tears. I sang loud as something moved in me with great joy and respect. Still to this day it triggers my memory of connecting with the Holy Spirit even though I didn't know it then.

Thorn: At ten years old, taller than my mom, I was a big girl, overweight, still growing rapidly, already five feet, ten inches tall. I had been wearing ugly big white orthope-dic shoes for years. Mom, on the advice of doctors, took me to UCLA Medical Center to have my glands examined for abnormalities. There were none found; I was growing as God had intended.

Rose: I continued to suck my thumb while carrying a fuzzy blanket as a sense of serenity. My eldest brother, Sam, added to my insecurities, pointing out my physical flaws and inadequacies. He and other mean kids at school teased me a lot about having black and rough skin on my neck and knees. He called it elephant skin. He also made fun of my singing and would say to me I could not carry a tune and that I sounded bad, so I stopped singing. Poverty was real in my house; the first of the month was happy times, plentiful, when the check and food stamps came. There would be food in the refrigerator and dinner on the stove. Mom did her best to meet the needs, although many needs were considered wants. My brother's father made a difference when he was not in prison. We learned how to make do. By the end of the month, we would put together what we had to eat. Our favorites were bread with butter, cinnamon and sugar toast, and fried bologna with mayonnaise.

Thorn: Remember I told you I would explain having daddy number 1 and father number 2? Well, this is it! Added with all the challenges I already felt from life, my mother told me when I was about eleven years old that a family friend that I had known as Uncle ST Jefferson thinks he is my biological father and we have to keep him a secret from my daddy, Otis. As a child, I found this so confusing. I did not understand how he could think he was my father or how I could have two fathers, and I hated having to keep the secret from my daddy, Otis. I was ashamed and resented my mother for this. ST was a friend of my mother's youngest brother. They served in the Navy together. I later learned he and my mother had one night together while he was home on a weekend pass from the Navy. He was a handsome, tall, quiet, and big-brown-eyed young Navy man. In his family, there was only him and an older sister, my aunt Barbara, and his mother, my grandmother, Lazzetta. His father remarried, and I did not know him. My aunt and grandmother would develop very close relationships; they would come to my house with her two girls about my age to meet me and to get a close look.

Rose: They believed I was his child because of a strong family resemblance. They loved me and cared for me as they did my aunt's four children. Both of them worked a job and owned their homes. My aunt Barbara had four children. I enjoyed the weekends that I would go to their house and stay with her, playing with my cousins. I learned to love them very much. There was always fun, with music dancing, and the neighbors on the block, the adults, would have alcohol. Occasionally, I would also stay with my grandmother Lazzetta, whom we called Butch because she didn't want to be called Grandmother. Maybe it was vanity. I enjoyed being with her. She was so graceful and proper. And being the only child felt good, what with getting lots of attention. My house was different. She taught me a lot about personal standards by the example she set. When I would stay with her, she would talk to me, teaching life lessons. Once, while I was dusting, she said, "Put some elbow grease on it," and smiling at the look on my face, expressing my ignorance, she explained, "Don't do a half-job in the same time you can do a complete job with a little more effort." I remember looking at her pictures of the many different places where she took cruises yearly and her beautiful jewelry and furs. Then she told me, "If you work diligently and take care of the things you have, you can have nice things too." My grandmother Butch was so conservative, tight even, concerning money, and so was my aunt Barbara and father number 2, ST. It was probably due to financial hard times they had survived and their respect for hard-earned money. They lived and taught not to waste. They would reuse paper towels, plastic, and aluminum foil. When they ate out, and even when Butch once was in the hospital, they would take home the butter and all the other condiments on the table. Aunt Barbara yelled at me once while I was making scrambled eggs for breakfast. I wasn't getting *all* the eggs out of the skillet, and she said, "Get *all* the egg by putting the hot eggs from the skillet into the bowl they were scrambled in, and the hot eggs would cook what was left in the bowl." My father number 2, ST, had all their ways and more. He was said to be downright stingy by those who knew him best. He would hurt me so much, living with much yet not contributing to me in poverty. An interesting fact about my father number 2: he was blood related to American gospel singer Mahalia Jackson and Heisman Trophy winner Mike Garrett.

Thorn: To compound that situation, my father number 2, ST, had a wife that objected to him having a relationship with me because she could not have children and was jealous of my mother's beauty. Dad had dated my mother and her at the same time but married her. She resented me and made it difficult for my father number 2, ST, and I to have a close relationship. The first time he took me to meet her at their house for the weekend, she was out for the evening. He and I had gone to sleep when I awakened by the sound of their argument and tousling. I heard her say, "Get that b——h out of my house!" I was afraid and confused. The following morning, she introduced herself with a pretense of acceptance as if she liked me, and that was the way the relationship went on to be. Any interaction with my father was always bittersweet, even though I spent time at their house on weekends and some holidays. She adopted a little boy from someone she knew to satisfy herself. My father already had a son two years older than me and was named after him. My father worked for Ford Motor Company, and his wife for the school district. They owned their home and lived very prosperously.

Thorn: The challenge that had the greatest effect was when our family learned that the illness my mom had suffered with for years was diagnosed as lupus, and the doctors at UCLA Medical Center gave her six months to live. I was devastated and felt a sense of hopelessness. My mama was my only security and the only consistent place of acceptance I had. I found comfort in her love for me and being able to express my love to her and know she was there for me unconditionally. Because of Mom's illness, she took lots of medication and slept all through the day and night. We were told to be quiet so Mom would not be awakened. After school, we played outside until the streetlights came on. Homework was not enforced. Home had little to no structure but no shortage of discipline. Mama did not attend any of my school activities, and that bothered me. I guess that was selfish of me since she really was sick. All I knew was the other children seemed so happy and proud to have their parents to share that time with, and I was alone. The older siblings did what they knew to manage the younger children and the house. But they had lives they were trying to figure out, being young adults just out of high school, working jobs.

Brokenness
Planted

With no support or guidance to help me process all that was going on in my life and no understanding of my own to make sense of the challenges and life circumstances and situations that were going on in my life, I learned to mask my feelings, trying to not add to the stress, and I became good at it. I learned to do and say all the right things. As I practiced manipulating and deceiving, those skills developed, became normal, and with them, my people-pleasing skills became who I was. Everyone would credit me with being "such a sweetheart." The thought was to do what I could to make others happy, and that allowed me to feel accepted, which determined my level of comfort and happiness. To be happy meant being comfortable, in control, without conflicts, and that was what meant the most to me. It became my non-stop pursuit. Maybe that was why I sucked my thumb with a fuzzy blanket until I was twelve years old, six feet tall, and two hundred pounds, to minimize my anxieties. I stopped sucking my thumb due to the teasing and started biting my nails. Mama tried to stop me. She would yell at me or say pretty girls had pretty hands and nails. That was such a far thought for me. I believed I was ugly and possibly unlovable. It was about this time in my life I started experimenting with mind-altering substances, due to the need of acceptance by my peers.

Thorn: My first high came in the form of Kool cigarettes and Coca-Cola. Older friends showed me that if I pulled from the cigarette long and hard and held it as long as I could, then took a swig of Coke then holding my breath just right, I would get a head rush. From there I started smoking marijuana, thinking it would make me more accepted by my peers. I also had curiosity of why it was so popular and what they were getting from it. When I smoked, I found I didn't feel so sad, inadequate, out of place, and afraid. So using mind-altering substances became the way I made life better and manageable. Because it made me feel good and the hurts were gone, if only temporarily. My beginning of an innocent child moved from love, faith, trust, and freedom to no love, fear, and slavery.

Thorn: At twelve years old, I was six feet tall and two hundred pounds and wearing a size 12 shoe. I did not feel like I fit in anywhere. I traded sucking my thumb for biting my nails and then added getting high. The structure of my family was dysfunctional, and poverty was real. Mom had serious health issues and an addiction to prescription medication.

Rose: We had a very close family; Mama insisted on it. Fighting among us siblings was not permitted. We all had a responsibility, to care for the sibling younger than we were. Everybody was expected to contribute to the needs of the house. My third older brother, Gerald, and I were very close. I needed the relationship, and the time he spent with me was so special. He was there for me more than any other was. He was in high school, and all the older sisters of my friends thought he was one of the cutest guys in school even though he was very shy. He had a job and car and would spend time with me, allowing me to hang out in his room. A couple of times, he took me to the movies with him. He was the only one who attended my graduations from junior high school, where I have no good memories, as well as high school.

Thorn: Mom was ill for many years, so she did not attend any of my school functions. She was in pain and slept a lot due to her meds and abuse. So neglect was real. Mom was not there emotionally, although she was physically. The older siblings stepped up. Mom's many years of being sick with lupus brought a cloud of pending doom in my mind. The thought of my mom dying added to my sense of instability, fear, and anxiety. That made me afraid and full of uncertainties. I felt like she was the only person who fully loved me and that I had to love. I thought, if she died, I did not want to live. I'm reminded of how important it was to me to show her how much she meant to me. I tried to communicate how much I loved her and express how I needed her, using songs and stories I would make up and hand-drawn pictures and cards. I was large in size but just a little girl.

Thorn: It was hard being me, and the older I got, the more difficult it became. I did not like myself and hated facing everyday life. I remember days like Halloween and going out with all the neighborhood kids trick-or-treating, and the person who opened the door looked out and said, "Aren't you too big to be trick-or-treating?" Everyone would laugh, and I'd drop my head in shame, wishing I could disappear. I was the child that was too *big* to do what the other children my age were doing all the time. That included junior high school, which was an awful three years where I did not fit in. I was a loner, trying to avoid being teased or having to fight. I was often teased and challenged by someone small. When I ignored them, it got worse. When I fought back, I was too "big" to be fighting them and made out to be a bully. I had a best friend, LW, who took the sting out of elementary and junior high school years. What stands out in my memory is during junior high school, being ashamed of my big, over-size body, fat, with stretch marks, like a woman after child-birth. Having to undress and shower at gym class, knowing my panties and bra were raggedy, giving my peers another reason to laugh at me. I'd rather take a fail. It was also in junior high, at thirteen years old, that I started my menstrual period. My mom had not prepared me for it. I didn't have the supplies needed, and everything I knew about it came from my friends. I believe we had very limited income, and that was why I did not get the supplies I needed. I made do.

Rose: A happier memory was my eldest brother, Sam, getting married and having his first son, my nephew Merrel. I spent a lot of time caring for him, introducing him to my favorite foods as he was able to eat, like pancakes and peanut butter and jelly sandwiches.

Thorn: The summer after junior high, I spent with my older cousin in Oxnard, California. She had moved to California from Kansas with her two little boys. Her hus-band was away in the military. I went to help her move into a house and to take care of the boys while she worked. I enjoyed the time with her, being away from home. My mind was distracted from those uncomfortable daily stressors. When I was with her, no one knew me or how old I was. I felt freedom and didn't think of home. I started keeping company with an older crowd, doing things that were more for adults. Now I was drinking more alcohol and smoking marijuana. It seemed to be more and more available to me.

Thorn: By the time I entered high school, my smoking was daily. My second eldest brother, Langston, represented the father figure in the house for the three younger siblings. He caught my friends and me several times getting high before and after school and scared us with verbal threats. I remember once, I went to my sister's house—she lived down the street from us—sneaking into my brother-in-law's weed box to get what I thought was mere marijuana, which was actually angel dust. That hallucinogenic high scared me away from that kind of high forever. I was so afraid of getting that high and having absolutely no control of myself I thought I was going to die. I called my cousin, and she helped me get a grip by having me lie still with a cold towel on my face. I didn't then, but I surely do now believe that cigarettes and marijuana are gateway drugs. I progressed in my substance abuse—speed, black mollies, powder cocaine—and I started smoking rock at twenty-three years old. When hitting the pipe, the goal of a good hit was described as hearing the bell ring, but following the bell, I sometimes would black out while the bell rang in my head. I did that a few times, but I was so afraid I would go only so far and stop so as not to go into the fullness of it and lose control. I made this false sense of control a habitual mindset, believing it was a good thing, being in control. Later in life, it was a real problem when I wanted to receive the filling and anointing of the Holy Spirit and God was doing something and it started to feel like I was losing control. It felt as if my mind and body were leaving me as I prayed with eyes closed and my arms raised. My legs were weak and giving away. I yelled out "Stop, I don't want it!" If it meant losing control, even to the Holy Spirit. And that's not good! You will see that I talk a lot about my need for control. Control and the need for it are caused by fear and hurt, cause and effect. I would tell myself that if I do this, this and that, controlling my surroundings, then that situation or event won't happen again and cause me that pain ever again. The only problem with that, I have found, is that in truth I don't have the ability to control anything or anyone but myself, and I didn't do that very well. So all I had was a false sense of control. My relationships were destroyed due to my unhealthy need to control; it is a very ugly characteristic and makes you hard to be around. Because I failed at controlling so severely for so long, until I surrendered and desired to walk after the Spirit, I received the help of God's Holy Spirit. His power showed itself in the fruit of the Spirit, discipline and self-control over my flesh, dying to my flesh (Gal. 5:22–23). The "fruit of the Holy Spirit" is a Bible term that sums up nine attributes of Christ Jesus and of a person living in accord with the Holy Spirit. "And those who belong to Christ Jesus have crucified the flesh with its passions and desires" (Gal. 5:24). I am most disappointed in myself for holding on to my old ways so long and denying the love and power of God waiting for me to come to the end of myself, with His arms wide open.

Rose: Those whom I spent most of my time within my developmental years were my neighbors. We had been friends since elementary school. They lived right next door, the four sisters. Some school friends we played on the volleyball and basketball team. My four cousins I spent weekends with, and of course my sister Vaughn. Vaughn and I were complete opposites, so much so that hardly anyone even knew we were sisters. LW and I became best friends as we attended the same elementary and junior high school. We would walk together or I'd get a ride from her family every day. My mom did not have a car. They owned their home, and her mom was a nurse, and her dad a lawyer. Her mom had remarried. LW was the youngest of three. She had a stable family structure, and her grandparents lived on the same property, in their own house, and assisted in caring for the children while her parents worked. She had much more than I did, in my view. I was grateful to be her friend. She always included me when she and her family went on outings. She and I remained best friends on into our adult life. Another good friend was JR. She and I met in my sophomore year and her junior year of high school. She actually was in the same grade as my sister Vaughn. Both of us were loners, me for being so big and tall and known to most as Big Sheron, and she had a drifting lazy eye and wore glasses. No wonder we became such close friends—we shared the need to be high. Some of the others that influenced my life were my aunt Barbara. She loved me and defended me from the wife of my father number 2, ST. She was creative and made beautiful pieces of furniture using gold leaf. She had an amazing voice and used to sing in clubs. She had a strong will and was fearless, with three children, and at fifty years old, she went back to college and got her bachelor's degree. My grandmother Lizzetta was a proper lady, beautiful, with class, surrounded by pretty things, with a strong work ethic. There was also my aunt Esther Jean, who was everything but nice; she was my mom's baby sister. She was six feet, two inches tall, a proud Amazon, a gangster in the full sense of the word. Dressed sharp always and would not back down from anyone, she did what she wanted, and that was usually breaking the law. Another influence I had was a drama teacher, Mrs. Forte. Her class was where I learned I was good at something. As long as I was behind a mask, pretending to be someone else, I was good.

Thorn: Still at sixteen, I was full of inadequacy; I saw no hope for my future. I wasn't smart in school. I hardly participated in class for fear of exposing how dumb I was and being laughed at. I did not study, nor did I do homework, and I hated it there. I was teased daily, called the Jolly Green Giant. I was shy and so insecure, still a nail-biter. Home did not encourage or support school attendance, studying or homework, and continued education, and neither was college ever spoken of. The future for me caused despair. I felt inadequate and incompetent in competing in life. I continued to grow, now at six feet, four inches tall and 240 pounds and size 13 shoes. I did not have fashionable clothes. I was still buying my clothes at Lane Bryant's, the fat-girl store. I felt ashamed of being poor, and every day I hated my oversize body and extremely knocked knees. I wore a heavy coat to school all day every day, regardless of the temperature, to hide behind.

Thorn: Therefore, my best thought was to drop out of school and have a baby. I did not have a boyfriend, but I knew I could get someone to "do it." I thought if I'd have a baby, I would have someone to love me, and that would make me happy, fulfilled, comfortable, and it would fix everything. I imagined I would get a welfare check to provide for us and be happy. I would not have to fear failing because I would be out of the race of life. When I shared my plan with my father number 2, ST, he said, "What about a father to help you with the baby, or a husband?" With great resentment toward him, I responded, "From what I have seen, I do not need a man to have a child. My mama did not need one to raise me or my brothers and sisters." Even though my mom was married multiple times, but not to her children's fathers. For me, I thought I would never have a man to love and care for me. I also talked to my brother Gerald, who had, at that time, gotten married. He and his wife, Debra, were expecting a child. Debra convinced me of what a bad idea that was. She told me they would share their baby with me. Anedra was her name, born the most precious little girl ever. Many nights when she was fussy, Debra would let me keep her and she would fall asleep on my chest. I spent as much time with her as I was allowed while still going to school. We loved each other. I met her needs, and she met mine. I can see now that I was a mess, an emotional handicap, lazy, looking for an easy way out. My fear and pain seemed to get better as my abuse of mind-altering substances became recreational.

Rose: My sister Vaughn was a grade ahead of me. At this point, she was in the twelfth grade and was very popular. The school started a girls' basketball and volleyball team. She talked me into joining. We both joined and played on the varsity teams and lettered. She was very good; I was just tall. I made new friends, and that expanded my social life. Vaughn was very athletic. She frequently played basketball on men's teams at the local community park. I played varsity two years. I was never good; I only played to be a center big man to guard the key, and I needed to be a part of something. Playing sports helped me come out of my shell some and corrected my being so clumsy. Vaughn and I were opposites; very few people at school even knew we were sisters. She was athletic, and I was clumsy. She was lean and stood six feet, two inches, was smart, and had hazel eyes and long honey-blond hair. I was dumb, fat, and stood six feet, six inches. There was nothing special about me.

Thorn: I believed if I were thin, I'd be attractive, happy, and I'd stand a chance at competing for a young man's attention. That was when I decided I wanted to lose weight, and I did. At that time, life seemed bearable, playing sports, engaging in social activities, and taking speed, which was then called cross tops, and black mollies. By the end of my senior year, I had lost eighty pounds. I decided I did not want to be a virgin anymore because I was as big as an adult and interacting with adults, and the only one among my peers that had not had sex. So I borrowed my uncle's car, although I didn't have a driver's licenses. I called Anthony and told him I was coming over. He had asked me several times prior, as we had been interacting at the club weekends that I was at my aunt Barbara's. I knew he liked me, and I liked him. He was older than me, quiet and tall. I gave my virginity away that night, February 12, 1975. There was no school, Abraham Lincoln's birthday.

Thorn: My good friend JR, shortly after graduating, started living with a man who was thirty years her senior that took good care of her. He was a widow, with five children, two already adults older than her, and three young children that lived with him. He had his own business, home, and drove a new Lincoln Continental. This was my senior year, and we were hooked up with everything we wanted. She lived the high life with expensive clothes, weekly hair and nail appointments, and a purse full of money and weed at all times. We thought we were the sh——t. Nobody could say anything to us. We stayed high, ran the streets, dressed to impress, having a nonstop party. We were spending time with an older crowd, very much out of place. We thought we were enjoying the good life. Before we were of legal age, my friends and I would go to the club on the weekend or hang out at some of our older friends' homes to get high. Dropping pills was happening at that time, like red devils, Percocet, and codeine. I didn't get down with them; my drug of choice was speed.

I felt like I'd changed from the ugly duckling to a beautiful swan. I was insecure and shy still as prom approached, but not as afraid. I had dreams of going and being a part of the "in" crowd. My sister Vaughn knew everyone and asked one of her friends, a nice-looking, older, and taller-than-me man from the team she played with at the park, to take me to the prom, and he agreed. Now I had a date. My grandmother Lazzetta, who was a professional tailor, made me the most beautiful, elegant sky-blue off-the-shoulder evening gown ever. My daddy number 1, Otis, gave me the money to buy the prom tickets. That night seemed to me like a dream come true, and my world changed. I was no longer the ugly duckling, but a beautiful swan. I received attention from men and women in awe of my height and beauty. People spoke nonstop on how beautiful I looked. That was the beginning of my end. I thought I had found that something that fulfilled me, my happy place, speed and being the center of attention. It seemed to make me comfortable in a way I didn't think was possible. Only in my new skin, life was better, I thought. I had found a sense of comfort and confidence; it was all about me. Like in the days of my early childhood, when my daddy number 1 was there and all the attention was on me. I began to change from shy to bold—you could not tell me anything! I went to the doctor for diet pills; what he gave me was a stronger form of speed, the street name black molly. I felt like I had found what was missing to make me who I wanted to be. I had come to see that I was becoming unteachable, self-centered, arrogant, full of false pride, and drifting away from the values, standards, and morals of my upbringing. Truly, practice makes perfect, if what is evil than evil, if what is good than good.

Vaughn went on to play professional basketball for the New York Harlem Queens and later enlisted in the United States Air Force. That is a perfect example of how different we were. I admired her so much. She was everything I was not and had all the character traits I wanted. I will admit, I was jealous of her.

I was full of false information. It was the last summer of my high school year, and by the skin of my teeth, I graduated with a C grade from all my teachers.

Thorn: One day, while my mother and I were out together, a man stopped us and told my mom I should be a model. He gave her his phone number on a card. He was from the John Robert Powers Modeling Agency. My mother took me there and, with her only income being a welfare check, signed a contract and made monthly payments for me to attend and train there because she believed in me. I started modeling on the weekends. That was where I learned to undress in front of unknown men without a thought. I was motivated to be as lean as I could, to get the best jobs. That influenced my substance abuse. Mama was pleased to see me lose weight and be all I wanted to be. Mom was the only one that always thought I was beautiful. My mom would see me slouching, smack me on my back, and say to me, "Stand up straight, hold your head high, and look at people right in their eyes and know you are in a class of your own. No one can compare to you." She would say, "You are so pretty it hurts people's eyes." I kept losing weight and coming out of my shyness and clothes.

Thorn: After high school ended, during the summer, I remember going to my mother one day to ask for money. She told me, "You don't get no more lunch money. You better do something to get a job or go to school." So I decide to be a respiratory therapist and registered in a career college. I was riding the bus downtown on the weekdays to college and back on Saturday to train at John Robert Powell Modeling. I felt good about what I was doing, but it was getting in my way of hanging out, getting high, and partying, so I stopped doing both of them. Mama came to me one day with mail from the County Welfare Office. She told me the mail was to find out, since I was not eighteen years old, if I was going to continue with school. Did she want to continue receiving monthly a check for me? I told her I didn't want to be on welfare anymore; I would get a job. Gaining understanding, I can say now I had no character. I was lazy, with no self-discipline or integrity.

Thorn: I became more uninhibited, bold, prideful, flirt, and sexually promiscuous. Men and sex became a game to me. I learned that all a woman had to do is take care of herself, be clean, smell good, show cared-for skin, have hair done, have white teeth, have beautiful nails and hands, and know just where to rub a man on the back of his head, and she could get everything he has. Mama taught her girls, "We are not prostitutes, but we don't have anything to give away." I would set out in a day to prove to my friends I could have any man I wanted, and as many as I wanted, and could get whatever I wanted from them. Men have been one of my biggest issues; daddy issues are real. Trying to fill the hole in my heart that my father left with another man, expecting him to make me whole, feeling adequate. When I looked back to acknowledge how I had been living, who I was becoming, and counted the men I had been intimate with, I could remember one hundred, but not all their names.

Thorn: I got a good-paying job working at Ford Motor Company, Parts Depot. I got the job through a man I had met while looking for work, Tony. He was the head union rep there. This place was full of men much older than I was. I did not have to do much work; they did my work for me. I would entertain them, telling them about my life and flirting with them by day, and I partied all night. It was at FMC where I learned many lasting lessons about life from some good people. Mr. Byrd told me, "Do whatever you want to while you are young. Take risks, because when you get old, you lose your heart." I had no idea what he meant then, but I have learned as I have aged the value of stability and security and freedom. Surely, losing one's freedom by going to jail is not an option. I made friends with many different cultures that enlightened my knowledge and opened me up to a completely new world. Mr. Dodo introduced me to the LA King Cobras motorcycle club. There, my sister Vaughn and I experienced nonstop parties and people who set out to enjoy life to the fullest. There I learned not to judge people. Nobody is all bad or all good. People are people, with differences, some rich, some poor. Mr. Earl was a very special, intimate, dear friend. Our relationship was real and lasted many years. Mr. Joe, we were very intimate, close friends. My family liked him a lot; he taught me the importance of good credit and to never date a married man because he will spend a lot of money on you; however, you will never be more than a toy for him to take off the shelf every chance he gets to play. I also learned from him that you could not judge a man by his height. Mr. Freeway, Mr. Rotor Rooter, special friends. Little Daddy, he put a ring on it. We got married and had a son. There was Touch and brother-in-law, Too Sweet. Ms. Patty, Mr. Ruck, and Castro. I met many that had a lasting impact on my development. These are just a few that stand out in my mind.

Thorn: Life was great. I realized money and my new self-image changed me, and not in a good way. I could do whatever I wanted to do. My self-image was high. I looked good, felt good, dressed the best, drove a new car, and had more than enough money to treat my mom to everything she wanted and gave my family members help too.

Thorn: My substance abuse was beginning to present itself as a problem. I not only used but, because of the abundance I was consuming, also sold it to boost my image and to absorb my cost. Now, with many new varieties of friends with various backgrounds, it was easy and I made more money. I felt important and wanted, like I fit and was somebody. I did not know or understand at that time the number one reason for substance abuse is hurt and fear. I thought I was having fun. However, the hurt and fear was why it made so much sense for me to abuse mind-altering substances. After years of denial and deception, I was making choices that went against all the values I was raised with. I had shame and guilt for behaviors I practiced on the daily. I looked for the hurt and fear that could have caused it. I started looking back and seeking why I made choices none of my siblings made. I could see that money and my new self-image changed me, and not in a good way. I was a deaf and blind man and a dead man walking (Matt. 13:13). Why did I, at twelve years old, smoke cigarettes and drank Coca-Cola at the same time, trying to get a head rush? There should not be any pain in a child's life that would cause this. That was the beginning of my end. Life seemed to be good, but not enough. Smoking marijuana made life seem better, and I needed to be high at all times to hide the way I felt. I used from the first thing in the morning and throughout the day. I would sink and lie about my using to avoid the truth about the severity of my using. I got worse! Abuse is when you use a thing that is meant for a purpose more to change or worsen/multiply, change the effect. I will speak about addiction latter.

Thorn: I was a victim of Satan's lies and schemes (John 8:44). Sin gives us the promise of pleasure, only to deliver pain. Satan created the bait, a lie that I was missing out on something good, promising pleasure, only to deliver pain. Out of fear I complied and swallowed the bait, hook, line, and sinker. "There is no fear in love. But perfect love drives out fear, because fear has to do with punishment. The one who fears is not made perfect in love" (1 John 4:18). God's love has no limits. He desires an intimate relationship with us.

> "The Lord is my light and my salvation—whom shall I fear? The Lord is the stronghold of my life—of whom shall I be afraid?" (Ps. 27:1).

So Deceived
Watered and Feed

Thorn: I thought I had it going on. According to the standards of my peers, I was winning, had it all, including my ticket to heaven when I died, because I went to church and believed Jesus is the Son of God and the Savior. I was grown and doing grown-up things. I was making big money on my job, partying, men at my east, west, north, and south. My main guy was a married guy I worked with. He made sure I didn't want for anything. He bought my first car, before I even had a driver's license, so I could meet up with him. He took me to expensive places and shopping, showing me off like a trophy. He had a lot of good ways, but no integrity. He was a short man, at five feet, six inches, and I was extreme at six feet, six inches. I learned to think of the value of quality over quantity while I was with him. Wherever we were, all eyes were on us. When we'd go to the movies, he would walk up to the ticket window and say, "We want two tickets," turn, and look up at me and say, "Right, Mommy?" and laugh at the look on everyone's face. He had lots of money, and the lifestyle to show it. He was a very sharp dresser, kept me draped, and drove a brand-new, big, shiny Continual. My entire family liked him. He didn't use anything and did not drink liquor. I was still living with my mother, with very little financial responsibilities. Life was great. So it made sense to me to move out and get my own apartment, because I was grown. I abused any kind of mind-altering substance to achieve an altered state of mind, to change my reality: diet pills, powder cocaine, and I moved on to smoking powder cocaine and then crack cocaine. It was called freebase. I found myself using narcotics such as opiates. I even tried smoking heroin. The only thing I did not do was inject drugs.

Thorn: At this same time in my journey, I was using so much I was not sleeping, was delusional, and during a routine visit to get more diet pills, the doctor admitted me for a seventy-two-hour hold in the hospital for a nervous breakdown. Seeking the answer to the question why. Why did abusing mind-altering substances feel right to me? I found it was because I was in so much pain deep inside. The pain was so deep I did not know where it began; it was as if it had always been there. I was in so much pain if I were not under the influence, it felt as if I were on the verge of tears, but if I began to cry, I would never stop. I continued to pretend I was fine and wore a mask, deceiving myself as well as everyone else. I lost who I was. I was addicted to many high-risk as well as self-destructive behaviors. With all this going on, what I did know was I needed someone to save me! I had everything the world could offer—beauty, money, men, many of them always the most attractive-looking, like Adonis, with lots of money, popularity, attention, a job, freedom. And it still was not enough to make me happy, except temporarily. I was loving the world and all that it could give. I had allowed people, places, and things to define who I was. I thought I was living my best life. But the truth was, I was so bound up. A slave to the things of the world. They controlled me. I was nothing without the people, places, possessions, and rituals, worldly idols and gods. It was obvious to those that knew me longest.

I will never forget when my cousin, who was also one of my best friends, told me I was a shallow bi———ch. I proudly strutted my shoulders, motioning, "And what's wrong with that?" Everything I had believed I would never have, I had. What I believed would make me happy did not.

Thorn: I needed a Savior. I was lost. My eldest sister, Renee, was the first one in the family to be saved and born again, Spirit-filled. She was the person the Lord used to bring me and my family to the awareness of what a relationship with Jesus Christ looks like in a person's life. I could see that she was different. Everything about her had changed from the sister I'd known my whole life. I accepted Christ Jesus as my Savior at the age of nineteen in the summer of 1977. That summer I thought I had it going on, that this world was mine, that it was all about me. I had been attending the same church I had been attending as a child with my father number 2's side of the family on most Sundays and realized I could not save myself and salvation was the only thing I didn't have. Although I was lord of my life, I believed on Jesus Christ as the Son of God and the Savior of the world, my Savior. It happened one Sunday at the end of the sermon. Pastor E. V. Hill of Mount Zion Missionary Baptist Church gave the benediction, asking if there was anyone who wanted to make a public confession of Jesus Christ as Lord and Savior and surrender their life to Him. I was standing, praying, eyes closed, and the next thing I knew, I was standing before the church. It was like an out-of-body experience. Pastor asked everyone that had come up front, if we wanted to surrender to Jesus, to pray this prayer after him, and I did. I was the first in the house Renee led to the Lord, to receive Christ as my Savior and be baptized. I guess she saw my pain through my mask. What I didn't know was, the Lord is an all-or-nothing God.

"For thou hast possessed my reins: thou hast covered me in my mother's womb. I will praise thee; for I am fearfully and wonderfully made: marvelous are thy works; and that my soul knoweth right well. My substance was not hid from thee, when I was made in secret, and curiously wrought in the lowest parts of the earth. Thine eyes did see my substance, yet being unperfect; and in thy book all my members were written, which in continuance were fashioned, when as yet there was none of them" (Ps. 139:13–16 KJV).

"For I know the thoughts that I think toward you, saith the LORD, thoughts of peace, and not of evil, to give you an expected end" (Jer. 29:11 KJV).

Thorn: You are always in motion, never at a standstill, either moving forward or backward. I only got worse. In the following four years, by the age of twenty-three years old, I had lost my firstborn son, Waymond, my marriage to Little Daddy, and my job with Ford Motors, and the drugs had a part in all of it. Also, drug abusers are known for their self-centered mentality. I was incapable of thinking about anyone else's needs over my own. I was the center of the universe, and everything was about pleasing me. It wasn't all Little Daddy's fault, but that didn't enter my mind at that time. I remember a conversation Renee and I had when I was so hurting and angry at Little Daddy, and Renee told me to turn him over to the Lord, to forgive him, and one day my heart would be changed and I would be praying for him to receive God's mercy and grace. And she gave me this scripture, Romans 10:13: "He that calls on the name of the Lord shall be saved."

I could not handle all the loss and sorrow. I was too sick and broken to accept any of the responsibility. So I did what hurting people do: hurt people! But I hurt myself trying to hurt Little Daddy, and I could find no relief from the hurt of what I thought was so unfair, and I had nothing but guilt, shame, anger, and regret about the loss of my first son.

Rose: My mom also surrendered, as Renee was instrumental in getting the entire household saved. To see God at work in my mother's life was nothing short of a miracle. Her life changed in so many ways. What stands out most was the healing she received. She was no longer abusing prescription medication, she no longer was in constant pain, and she was no longer bound to the bed. She started attending Mount Zion and building an intimate relationship with Jesus. She was in the Word, served in the church as a part of the prayer team, and helped feed the hungry twice weekly at the church's facility, called the Lord's Kitchen. She was so energized and helpful wherever, however she could. She was instrumental in starting a weekly small group study where she lived. God changed her life. Remember, doctors had given her six months to live twelve years ago, and the Lord spared her life and gave her a long, good life (Deut. 30:19, 5:33; Prov. 9:11, 3:1). Mama lived forty-two more years before she went home to the Lord. The medical doctors were amazed. She is the longest-living lupus patient on record.

Whose report will you believe? Will it be the Lord's or man's?

Isaiah 53:1 says, "Who has believed our report? And to whom is the Arm of the Lord revealed?"

Romans 3:4 says, "Let God be true and every man a liar."

Psalms 1:1–3 tells us, "Blessed are those who do not follow the advice of the ungodly, but delight in the law of the Lord."

The Lord used me to lead my little brother, Shelly, to Jesus. My family attended the church Renee was now a member of, Mount Zion Missionary Baptist Church, with Pastor E. V. Hill. I know now that there are no coincidences in a child of God's life. Mount Zion just happened to be the same church that my father number 2, ST, and his family had been members of since he was a child. The same church where my grandmother Lazzetta and his sister, my aunt Barbara, and cousins attended. I accepted Christ at the age of nineteen, while actively involved in this ungodly lifestyle. I thought of receiving Christ and His salvation as my guaranteed ticket to heaven. I felt like I had everything life could offer. I was smart, pretty, cool, popular; I had a good job, making big money, and anything that a man had, I could get. I thought I had all that I needed, except I did not have the salvation, which I thought of as the assurance of heaven when I died. Although I was still lord over my own life. I went to church on Sunday, but I lived like hell Monday through Saturday. I felt like life was great. I had everything. I responded to the gospel, confessed Jesus Christ as my Savior, and was baptized unto forgiveness of sin for assurance of heaven when I died, at Mount Zion Missionary Baptist Church, under the shepherd Pastor E. V. Hill. I felt like life was complete. But I was still lost in life. I did whatever whenever I wanted and was all about pleasing myself. I observed and felt jealous of those that accepted Jesus as Savior and Lord at the same time I did. Their lives were changing, blessed mightily, growing, and successfully accomplishing goals of life. They were prospering with accomplishments, marriage, children, and gifted, delivered, and being used to do great things in the name of

Jesus. My perception of life was so twisted I thought I was winning; I was in control of every person, place, and thing that was in my world. I was accountable to no one. "I was grown." Making lots of money, I gave my mom anything she wanted. I bought myself a brand-new 1977 Mercury Elite car and moved into my own apartment.

I was prideful and arrogant. I thought I was the most attractive woman around. Renee was attending a weekly Bible study in Pasadena at the house of her best friend who was married to a Motown Record producer. Renee would invite me every Saturday to come to the Bible study, motivating me with names of entertainers and famous people that attended. When she started naming names, she got my attention; I was intrigued, so I went. One of the most famous, attractive, legendary Motown singer/songwriter/producer in the industry attended with his wife. I went, and he could not keep his eyes off me, despite his being there with his wife. After the study, during the meet-and-greet, he walked up to me, introduced himself, and stated, "Lady, you have boomed me." We talked for a moment, and he asked for my telephone number. Of course, I gave it to him, and by the time I had reached home, he had called. The message was, "S——s calling you." In excitement, I helped her recognize who he was. She identified him as "that squeaky-voiced man." Following, we met at the Beverly Hills Hotel a few times after Bible study, indulging in smoking good bud and sex. I was young and so impressed by his status and the fact that he chose me. I thought that made me special, increasing my self-image. My thinking was so twisted! We met up a few times, and by the end of our time together, he bought me a Longines diamond watch, and I had memories as a trophy. Again, you could not tell me anything.

This world was mine. I could have anything I wanted, and if a man had it, I could get it from him. Awkward, afraid, ugly Sheron was no more. That winter I went to Oklahoma for the funeral of my grandfather, my mother's father, on my way there, while standing in the Los Angeles Airport, heads above all others, as always dressed sharp in a white maxi coat and boots with four-inch heels, I locked eyes with the only other person whose head was above the crowd, a basketball legend. As KJ made his way over to me, he told me how stunning I looked. I was overly excited and embarrassed myself talking to him about how tall he was. I said the same aggravating statements to him people had said to me all the time. When I reached my grandmother's house, one of the first things she said to me was, "Sheron Ann, I never thought you would be a pretty girl. You have changed from an ugly duckling to a beautiful swan." Once again, my exceptional beauty was confirmed. While in Oklahoma, I was the focus of attention, being from Cali; one of my admirers even proposed marriage, though he was killed a few months following. While there, I indulged and continued to get high, drinking alcohol and smoking weed even at the funeral. My behavior was shameful.

Upon my return to California, hanging out at the right places, I caught the attention of a World Heavyweight boxer, MA, who was in the company of actress JK. He said, "Oooh, girl, you sure are a pretty thing." Attention like that fed my ego every day. Being told I was beautiful by men on that level made me feel more special. My outer was attractive, but there was nothing pretty on the inside, and I thought that was enough to live life satisfied. No more low self-esteem and fear of rejection from my past. I was turning into much worse. Remember my sick thinking, saying that things were good and I was happy when I was the center of attention and the world revolved around me? I thought all was well when my perceived needs were met and were priority over everything else. When I was receiving and giving physical and emotional connection, I felt secure and valued. What seemed to be stable and consistent was my comfort zone. Also, when I was in control, I felt valued, important, loved, and I had a sense of well-being when things were going as I believed they should. Psychology has labeled this disorder the king baby syndrome. Although my experience in this comfort zone was very short-lived, temporary, always needing more, which is where my belief of what is good and what is bad, if I am happy or sad, is based off. That was what I defined as happiness. When life is all about me, partying all the time, traveling, abusing recreational substance, having sexual promiscuity, no accountability, and where familiar is comfort. More money than I had ever imagined that gave me a sense of control and being self-sufficient. Money and control were usually coming from selling drugs, marijuana, and cocaine by the pound and from gifts from men. I did not see a problem in immoral or illegal behavior.

The Need for Control

Took Root

Thorn: When Little Daddy asked me to marry him, I was living a dream come true, but I was not ready for marriage. I was too immature, wounded, and broken for my marriage to stand a chance. At twenty-one years old, in 1980, I married Little Daddy. He was an exceptional person, intriguing, fun, and with lots of personality and interest. He rode with the King Cobra Motorcycle Club and owned his own tow truck for work, drove an impressive Lincoln Continental, was flashy and popular and a good hustler, and was motivated. He had what I needed to fulfill my feeling of inadequacy. He had a very comforting but strong personality. He was physically attractive, with strong, manly ways, although he was shorter than me by six inches. He worked hard for the money and had lots to show for it. His motto was, if it's not about money, it's not worth his time. He was a fun person to be around, except for when his money was not right. Little Daddy had good family values, raised by his mother as the second eldest son of three boys and one younger sister. He was a very motivated, self-driven man with a criminal history, willing to take risk, fearless when it came to making money. He tried to balance life, work, play, and church. To me he seemed too good to be true. When he started showing his interest for me, I thought it was a game he was playing to impress his motorcycles brothers. Proving that he could get the sexy young Amazon that was about having things that all the men wanted. The King Cobra clubhouse, where we partied together weekly, was where we met. We dated for six months, and then he asked me to marry him. I thought I would call his bluff, but to my surprise, he had bought rings and set a date. Little Daddy was five years older than me. He had a very private side about himself, trusted and let very few get close, a great person with a strong personality, and a lot like myself. We went to Las Vegas to get married, and Vaughn went as our witness. Renee and Vaughn gave the reception. It was beautiful. It was on November 10, held at Marla Gibbs Memory Lane Club. Our theme was "Forever Mine," taken from the O'Jays song. We were happy, and it felt like a storybook love. My eldest sister, Renee, who is an amazing seamstress, made two outfits for me. To make my entrance, I wore a long white fitted satin dress with no sleeves, a scooped neck, and a red satin sash around my hips. For the after-party, a white satin lounge pants set and a strapless top with a red sash at the waist. Little Daddy wore a white suit with a red shirt and white tie with pocket hankie. All our family and friends were there. Our wedding dance song was "Freak of the Week." We started out good, and I thought we were a ride-or-die team for life. I was ready to go all the way. To show him how invested in us I was, he wanted another tow truck, so I put the money in on a new tow truck for him. What had happened was, I believe Little Daddy, being a manly man, traditional, old-school, thought I would be a stay-at-home wife and take care of her man, a be-happy-in-the-background kind of wife. But my issues of inadequacy, fear of rejection, pride, using haughtiness, using sexuality, and materialism to hide behind would not let me.

If only I could have said what I meant and not what I felt. We married in November, and by February, Valentine's Day, we were not feeling the love; we did spend the day together, but not the night. He went his way with his club brothers to hang out with and left me at home. I went with my ex, who always said I should have been his wife. Little Daddy and I had a huge argument with lots of hurtful words followed. It was our first. I left our home hoping he would come after me, but he did not. At my mother's advice to go back after a week, she told me, "A woman is never to leave her home." I went back and caught him in bed with a woman. We got back together after realizing I was pregnant.

Thorn: I would learn to listen to authorities one day. Early in my pregnancy, I was in a car accident just a block from the house. The insurance company totaled my two-year-old car and paid me nothing because that month's payment was still in Little Daddy's pocket. After the accident, I started having some difficulty with my pregnancy. I was about four months pregnant when the doctor took me off work and put me on total bed rest. Little Daddy worked and provided well; I didn't have to worry about a thing. Family members came to care for me daily.

Thorn: The San Diego Cool Jazz Festival was an annual event that we attended together in the past was approaching. Little Daddy was riding with the club as usual. I told him I did not want him to go because I could not go. I was not going due to the doctor's bed rest orders. He went anyway, and I said no to the doctor's orders and went anyways. Six weeks later, on August 5, I delivered prematurely. Waymond Rashard was one pound, twelve ounces. Little Daddy and I were together. We held our son briefly after delivery, and then he was taken to Children's Hospital because his lungs were not fully developed. Little Daddy stayed with him there. He lived one day. The pain was unspeakable, and so many emotions crossed my heart and mind. I wanted a baby so bad, but because of my own selfish ways, he was gone. There was no way to find comfort. I could not find a moment in time or a place in space anywhere I went, and nothing I would do separated me from the pain. Little Daddy stepped up big to organize the funeral. He handled everything and never spoke his feelings. I had so many tears, my heart was broken, and I felt full of guilt, shame, and anger. I withdrew after the funeral and painted the whole apartment in two days, crying and painting, while my breasts filled with milk and there was no baby to feed. I felt all alone and thought to myself, *Nobody cares why you are crying.* I convinced myself, *Stop crying. What good is crying? It will not change anything.* That was what I did. I sucked up all my thoughts and feelings, withdrew, and went inward. I have learned to call this running away instead of facing life's hurts.

Thorn: Three months later, after the funeral, Little Daddy and I had become more distant, individually avoiding dealing with our hurt, grief, and sadness. He and I were fighting because he wanted to spend time with his motorcycle brothers and not me; that was his way of coping. He was going on another motorcycle run and did not want me to go. We argued, and I told him that if he left, we were done. Love didn't live there anymore, and he left anyway. I had the locks changed, and two weeks later, while I had returned to work, he broke into the apartment and took all the furniture. I could have killed him; I don't take loss well. I myself was caught up in many self-destructive behaviors. I turned inward, angry, hurting, seeking relief from the pain, and to get back at him, I got a gun, slept with all his friends while abusing drugs. I turned to every high-risk, self-destructive behavior I knew. I was immature, self-centered, unwilling to submit, prideful, arrogant, broken, and insecure. My thinking was all messed up. I thought I could do anything he could do better, including cheating, partying, and hustling. What I did not understand was that at the end of the day, he would still be a man, and I had reduced myself to less than a woman, a filthy whore. I did not know it, but I was destined to fail. I had too much junk and baggage from my past to be a good wife and mother or to receive the good things that the Lord had for me. I was so afraid of being hurt, rejected, and abandoned. I was self-absorbed, and I could not freely love or be loved. On the outside, I seemed flawless, but on the inside, I was so broken and dark. This marriage did not stand a chance. It was my dream to be married to a man like him and have children. Until the end of our marriage, the relationship was ugly, full of hatred, and all communication stopped. One would be talking but not being heard by the other; we completely shut down. I hired a lawyer and filed for divorce. Little Daddy told the both of us that he would never give me a divorce. The judge ruled in my favor, and I got everything I asked for. I was able to get my maiden name back. Financially, he owed me and was to pay for the divorce, but he told my lawyer he would not pay; he did not want a divorce, would never divorce me, and would never marry again. He had chosen his wife. I left the court having been given a divorce. It was done. Our marriage lasted 360 days because of my brokenness, being immature and needy, with unaddressed issues.

Thorn: The things I did for the high! Deep in pain, I did not want to feel, but I could not find any escape. I went back to work and was in need of a car. I had lost mine due to the accident. It just so happened that one of Little Daddy's friends I was seeing gave me a car, a 1969 Lincoln Continental, newly painted money-green, metallic, to match the convertible top and leather interior. It was clean! He had taken it from his wife, and I did not know that, and it didn't matter to me. One day, while I was at his shop, she introduced herself and stated she had been looking forward to meeting the one whom he had given her car to. We became friends. She was an in-the-closet bougie crack smoker. They both made lots of money. She had her own business and possessed lots of nice things. At first, I thought it was strange he would encourage the two of us to become friends; he also financed our times together, lunch dates and such. She told me that the reason he liked us being friends was that he was such a sexual freak, and although he didn't use drugs, she and the women he befriended, giving them gifts, were his playthings when crack was being used, and he got his sexual needs met.

Caught in a Downward Spiral
##

I did not recognize it, but things were changing. My cocaine usage increased, along with more smoking marijuana, taking diet pills, and drinking alcohol. It was during this time that I had my last cry. I convinced myself and believed the lie that it did not help and it made me look weak and vulnerable. I felt so defeated and weak I told myself to be strong and never cry again. I would not feel pain again, and I used mind-altering substances and self-destructive behaviors to escape the feelings.

Thorn: You might be wondering, as I was, Was I having fun yet? When I began, I thought it was fun, but now I was running from something. I was so lost in darkness. You know what they say, the way to get over a man is to get a new one. Well, at this time, my cousins introduced me to some guys they had met from the East Side, which was known as the Dirty Bottom. It was known for the hustlers, thugs, and its hangouts. The spot we frequented weekly was called the Buck House, a gambling house. I connected with one of the guys, WC. The after-hour clubs became our new stomping grounds. We became very acquainted with another level of streets, ruthless, self-centered ungodliness. After the many losses I'd had—car, my baby, marriage, and finally, the job—

another boyfriend, who was also a drug abuser, introduced me and school friend JJ to smoking crack cocaine called free-base, and it was on from there. Another man with a body like a god's and great sex, a man with style, a roughneck, with all the signs, including a criminal record. He was a hus-tler; when he hit a lick, he hit big. A showboat and attractive dresser, and did I mention the sex? That was a major addic-tion for me also. My sister Vaughn was living with me in the apartment after Little Daddy had left, and on this particular day, after spending the night at my place, my new boyfriend, WC, dropped me off at work and kept my car so he could get new tires put on for me. When I returned home, one of my thick and heavy, expensive gold ropes with a flying-eagle charm was missing from my room. I remember it being there when he and I left that morning, and he told me he had not been back since. Now, Vaughn had a history of stealing and lying. I blamed her for the stolen piece of jewelry. She and I fought about it, and following the fight, I told her everything I had, she was welcome to; she did not need to steal from me. And I gave her access to my bank account. She never changed her story, so I left the issue of my missing gold rope alone.

Without a conscience, I dated more men than I can remember, more than two men at a time, intimate with them all. WC went to prison, locked down at Peter Pitch Correctional County Facility. I would get out of bed Saturday morning with one person and go visit WC for the day. Even worse, for the visit, which was my real motivation for going, I would roll 150 pinhead-size marijuana joints. First, I would stop on the freeway alongside the fence of the facility and throw a bundle of 50 over the fence. He had another inmate he paid that worked that area get them to him. I would bring the other two bundles of 50 into the prison on me. I would go into the restroom and place them in an opening under the sink, where he had told me and another inmate that worked that area would get those to him. He sent the money he made to me; I would put some on his books, but of course, the majority went to me. That was how deep into darkness my lifestyle was. I not only took penitentiary chances with my freedom, but I also did not see it as wrong. I made multiple high-risk decisions while under the influence.

Thorn: I was making such poor choices. We dated again after he was released from prison, until he tried to rob me on my birthday so he could buy crack to get high. The last time we saw each other was on my birthday. Once again, hoping and waiting for Little Daddy to call me back with the plans he said he had prepared for the evening, and he never did. So I settled when WC called, and I thought I'd show Little Daddy he didn't stop me. WC and I were already at the end of the relationship; he just was not good for me or to me anymore. But it was my birthday, and I wanted to be taken out to celebrate and get my party on. So I gave him another chance. After all, he offered the best sex, and he dressed well, a body like Adonis's and a new yellow Corvette he said he bought for me, his fly yellow girl. He had no job, just a hustler that stole from jewelry stores. When we were dating, I was a bad girl making a name for myself on the streets of the bad side of town in after-hour gambling clubs, rebelling against all expectations, associating with those of no honor or integrity like myself. I was mimicking my mom's baby sister, my aunt Esther Jean. I truly was caught up in a downward spiral, being pulled deeper and deeper. Staying home on my birthday was not an option, so when he called, I said yes. Because I could not trust what he might do based on prior experiences, I told him I would drive. When I arrived at his house and my fabulous silk outfit draped in baling from head to toe, including the ten-thousand-dollar, two-carat, emerald-cut baguette diamond he had given me, he was not dressed and asked me to come in and have a drink. I should have followed my feelings then and left. I knew he was high, but I had never seen anyone like that. He started asking me for money, just $20 he needed, with some lie he was telling about someone being on their way over to bring him money he was owed. I gave him $20, and he said he would be right back. I waited. Now, it was getting later and later, and when he did return, he was on one and there was darkness all over him. He begged for more money, and I told him no and moved toward the door. Then he demanded I give him money or a piece of jewelry that he would get back to me later. He got a large kitchen knife and threatened me. "No way. Just kill me," I said. "I am out of here." I pulled the collar of my coat high and tightly around my neck so he could not get my gold necklaces. I put my purse on my shoulder and pushed my way out the door as he was blocking and threatening to stab me. My body was halfway out the door when he cut the straps of my purse and took it. The keys to my car were in my purse, but I kept walking. It was midnight, dark and quiet. I walked down the middle of the street, yelling for help, heading toward the main street, where there were cars and lights. He continuously told me to go back to the house while trying to get his hands inside my coat collar and on my jewelry as I fought to defend myself. As we walked, we argued and struggled. I reached inside my pocket, and there was a box cutter tool I used at my job. The next time he grabbed for my collar, I stuck the razor in his hand and cut him deep and long. When the night air hit his hand, he realized he was cut and bleeding but could not see. He left me alone and went back to his house. I made it to the corner of the major street and started flagging down someone for help. Two young women picked me up and took me to the nearest police station. There I made a report. One of the officers made the remark he could tell that I did not belong on that side of town. He asked what I wanted them to do; I said, "Get my purse back for me." The officer asked if there was anyone I would like to call before they took me back to his house for my purse. I thought of my eldest brother, Sam, who lived nearby, and called him. I explained to him what had happened, and he asked if I was sure that I was finished with that man, and if not, I should not get him involved. Sam said, "But if you are finished, I am on my way to his house, and the police better get there before I do." The police did get there first; they went into the house and brought him out. WC stood there with his arm over his head, a bloody towel wrapped around it, crying, "Baby, you didn't have to cut me." The police gave me my purse, told me to leave, and called an ambulance for him. Sam and I left. That was the last time I saw WC. I put myself through all that just because of rebellion and because the sex was good. I was trying to fill the emptiness in myself, by pleasing myself. I now know that is what abuse and addiction is all about, self-pleasing selfishness to cover up pain and fear.

I was told about an encounter by a mutual friend of Little Daddy's and mine that almost caused somebody to get shot because of me. This friend, Little Daddy, and another friend went out to breakfast and just happened to sit in a booth with their back to a group of guys. While waiting for their server, minding their own business, Little Daddy overheard the guy behind him talking about his freaky sexual encounter with a bad six-foot, six-inch Amazon. Little Daddy turned to the man and asked him to keep his voice down; he didn't want to hear that. The man responded that he didn't care. "Then don't listen." By that time, Little Daddy's friends also overheard what the guy was saying. Little Daddy was hot and stood up, saying he would shoot this m——f. One of his friends grabbed him and walked him out of the restaurant, while another friend with him told the guy talking about his night with me that he was talking about that man's wife and that they shouldn't still be there when he came back. So he and his friends left.

I was living wild and reckless. I was pleased to hear that Little Daddy was bothered by my sleeping around. It made me feel like he still had love for me too. I wanted him to care and hurt like I hurt. Hurting people hurt people.

Living to Die
Branches

Thorn: After I had returned to work. My addiction was so strong I got high from morning until night. At work, during the breaks, and throughout the day, wherever I happened to be, until late into the night. I took off work often and was late a lot of days due to the all-night partying. I once called my house after work. My friend JJ was staying with me. She answered the phone and told me she was smoking crack. I was speeding to get there before she smoked it all when an ambulance turned on its siren, driving in the lane in front of me. I know I should have pulled to the right and stopped, but the urges and anxious feeling to get to the high were overwhelming. So what I did was pull to the left to go around the ambulance. When I went left, they went left, and I rear-ended the ambulance. The police came, my car was towed, it was a big mess, and when I did finally get home, the dope was gone. Only a crackhead would race an ambulance.

The Ford Motor Company had a big layoff and offered an early retirement payout, and I took the money. I did not know it then, but that was a big mistake. With my being unemployed, with no structure in life, everything got worse because of freebase. Crack cocaine introduced me to a whole other level of addiction, self-centeredness, and darkness. I see it now as God allowing me to have my own way, showing me my insanity, and my conscience became more quiet. He made it evident how far my ways were from His ways, and how far I would go. I see how God allowed and brought me through that time for the plan He has purposed for my life. All buildings must have a foundation. "Unless the Lord builds the house it cannot stand!" (Isa. 59:1). The taller the building, the deeper and wider the foundation must be.

Thorn: I tried to run away because I did not want to change. It was after I stopped working that the awareness that my life was in trouble happened. I attempted to run from the truth, only running deeper and deeper into self, sin, and immoral behaviors. I was so lost I thought joining a traveling magazine company that promised executive positions and travel would take me away from my problems. By joining this door-to-door traveling magazine sales company, where we lived two people to a room in a low-budget, motel-earning commission. Every morning, vans of workers would be picked up and dropped off in designated commercial areas of the city. Each person would walk opposite sides of the street, eight hours a day, competing to sell the most magazine and receive the recognition of top salesperson of the day. The aim was to be salesperson of the month. The vans would return at the end of the day to pick us up to return us to the motel, where we would meet, turn in any money, buddy up with our roommate, and go eat at a fast-food restaurant. We stayed in that city until we had covered the primary areas, and then we would move on to another city. Those who had sold the most subscriptions would be allowed to move to other states. I did that for about sixty days. I missed my life. I realized that I could not move far enough from myself. The problem was still there; wherever I went, there I was. I was the problem. The change I was looking for was not going to happen; I did not want to stop. I was not really making any money. And I hated what I was doing. I was not able to be in control to do what I wanted to do, and that was what made me most uncomfortable. I had my own car parked at home while I waited for someone else to pick me up and drop me off, which just didn't work for me. All my expensive shoes and clothes were designer and made for the clubs and were being mistreated. I felt like I was not like "those other people." What I wanted to do was get high, have sex, and party. I learned that changing scenery and zip codes did not change me. The message I got from this is that you can run but you cannot hide from yourself. I brought my old habits with me. I identified my pattern of behaviors as a runner and a deceiver with a lack of discipline. I went back to what I did best, enjoying the darkness.

Thorn: My little brother, Shelly, was a victim and almost a casualty of my ungodly, unhealthy lifestyle, values, and beliefs. I was training him to be my right-hand man at fifteen years old; he looked older than he was. He was six feet, five inches tall, with a solid, muscular body. He dealt my drugs at school, marijuana and powder cocaine. He had complete access to my drug stash. I lived just a few blocks between my mom's apartment and his school, and he and his friends would come over during lunch break and after school to get as high as they could. On weekends, when things were happening, I dressed him as my equal, suited up, so that his age was not noticeable. He was my driver when I would go met someone to deal, attend a social gathering, or go to a party. I trained him to pimp, using women that were about that life to teach him. His personal goal was to make enough money by the time he graduated high school to buy a radio station. He had bought in to the lifestyle completely. Thank God things started going wrong with him at school because of the lifestyle and his indifferent attitude. This brought him to the attention of the school, and then Mom. So that he would graduate, he was bused out of the area. He and his girlfriend had serious problems due to their just being children given adult privileges, behaving as if they were adults. This would have killed my mother, or she would have killed us if she had known what I had done to her baby boy. I did not just make devastatingly destructive chooses for my life but also almost took my little brother out too. I played a role in the destruction of others' lives. JJ, my friend from high school, was there when I was introduced to freebase by the friends of my cousins. At my apartment, she and her baby, my godson, were staying with me. It was all bad from there for both of us in every way, including our friendship. She fell for it harder than I did. She was caught up in it longer than I was. I am sorry for the influence I had in her using, although we each made choices. I am so grateful for what I was saved from. I also introduced another dear cousin to crack cocaine. In my sick thinking, I thought I would help her; she was smoking PCP, neglecting her little boy, putting herself in danger with being raped, possibly jail, and CPS. I thought crack was the better of the two. She got stuck in the madness, and it was not better, just different, with the same consequences. I also introduced my best friend from junior high school to the pipe. She loved it and got turned out. My friend was lucky and was caught very quickly using. She started getting high without me, and one night, while in the park, smoking, she was arrested. Her family bailed her out of jail. She was given a fine to pay that she could afford and ordered to attend ninety meetings in ninety days of Cocaine Anonymous, and the case was dropped. That whole situation was a blessing. The fact of her using was brought to light quickly, and she came to her senses before she was stuck in that addiction. As I and my cousin and friend did not get caught, we continued in a life of decay and destruction.

The worse I got, the more I pretended and deceived myself into believing I was okay, that I could quit anytime I wanted, and I was not hurting anyone but myself. I went so far as to stop feeling anything totally. I was no longer human. Going to church but still lord of my own life and in control. I thought, as long as I had beauty and money, I had followers that loved me. At this point, I was so self-centered, materialistic, and shallow. I would live like hell all week, doing the worst imaginable things, and go to church on Sunday. I was deceiving myself and others to believe I was a good person. I could talk the talk and had others coming to me for prayer and spiritual counsel. All I knew to tell them was what I had heard from the preacher's pulpit, because I had not read the Bible for myself. I did not know, nor did would I believe at that point, how low I would go. I still had some standards and limits, although superficial and egotistical. My image and what others thought about me, how I looked to them, was all that mattered to me. As long as I was the best at whatever the deed was, I did it the biggest, always competing and comparing in my mind. I was invited to all the events because I set the standards, I brought the party, and I was the beautiful Amazon that would take your man, fly, and ghetto, fabulous, scandalous b——ch that did not care about anything and anybody but self-gratification. I dated married men with money and too much to lose so that there was no commitment and I could have things my way. I did what I wanted to do. I had an aunt, my mom's baby sister, named Esther Jean, that was somewhat of an epic legend in the streets and my idol. She had earned a reputation as a bad, fearless gangster that was fabulous in the streets, and that was who I was going to be like. But God had other plans for me as I made all the wrong choices. He did not give up on me, as hard as I tried to do life my way; He kept tiring to get me to turn from my wicked ways and turn to Him. After the death of my son and the end of my failed marriage, the loss of my possessions, job, relationships, and self, I was hurting and found it difficult to manage life. My sister Renee shared a scripture that stuck with me: "Whomever calls upon the name of the Lord shall be saved" (Rom. 10:13). She also told me then that one day I would look back on this time with a completely different heart toward the situation. I felt the pain of rejection, shame, betrayal, guilt, and loss, and I blamed Little Daddy for it all. I put on a mask to distance myself from the truth, to avoid feeling any hurt. I was self-absorbed, pleasure-focused, and partying all the time was my new motto.

That summer, I was shot in the butt with a 9mm gun. Every Saturday, there was a concert held at the park, where my girls and I would join all the other cool people, consume alcohol, do weed, hook up, all while listening to music and dancing. One particular Saturday, I ran out of Zig-Zag rolling papers while at the park. There was a store next door and a hole in the fence where I could take a shortcut. I was dressed in my cute summer attire, with tight white jeans and a midriff blouse, drawing all the attention, as usual. Taking the shortcut through the fence to the store, I bent over in half, being six feet, six inches tall, to go through the opening, a hole in the fence. Behind me to my right, I observed three guys talking. I had just passed them a few feet away when one of them pulled his 9mm and started shooting the guys he was talking to. The first bullet missed, hit the ground, ricocheted up, and landed in my butt cheek. It could have been worse. My head and neck and all the vital organs between my butt and head were at the same level. I ran for cover and felt something burning like fire deep within. I started calling for help and shouting repeatedly, "I have been shot!" First, the police responded, then the ambulance. They cut my sexy white jeans off while sexual comments were made by the ambulance attendants because I was not wearing underwear. They took me to the hospital, and the doctor did not remove the bullet, stating it would be best and cause less of a problem to leave it. The message I received from that incident was that God had a plan for my life, and that was why it was not more serious; I could have been killed. God was quietly calling for my attention, but I kept running away. Realizing that but for His mercy I could have been killed. As I look back, I see God was gently calling me, but I thought I knew what was best for me and kept going my way. It was at the hospital that I could see God stopped me in my tracks and had my full attention. I saw what my way had gotten me. Still, that didn't stop me. I have learned that nothing happens without God's permission to a child of God and He has a plan for my life. My downward spiral continued, but my perspective was, my life was Fantasy Island. It was my world, and I was off the hook. My favorite quote was "Party all the time, party all the time." Now abusing drugs and also selling and being totally involved in the lifestyle. Living by the principles my mom taught me that a woman's beauty is her greatest asset, if she uses it right. Therefore, growing out of that inadequate, insecure stage I had lived as a child, now into a brick house, an Amazon, a trophy, beautiful from head to toe. I was using men and being used by them, of course for the right price. I behaved as if I could have any man I wanted; the list was long, and they would give me anything I wanted. God was still pursuing me.

The following summer, on a Saturday morning, I went jogging in a rocky, hilly area with a guy I had been seeing who was into health fitness. We ran uphill, and on the way down, I became fearful, suddenly remembered how deathly afraid of heights I was, and began tumbling down. The only things I remember are that he tried to catch me, fear, and pain, until I blacked out. When I came to, the fire department was on the scene, asking me questions. They took me to the hospital, where my mom and Little Daddy were called to come. The look on their faces told me that it was really bad. When I asked for a mirror, the doctors began explaining that the injuries would take some time to heal but they would go away. They told me that I would have black eyes, my eyebrows would grow back, and once the swelling subsided, they could assess my nose. The biggest issue was my chin. I was told that it might require cosmetic surgery to remove scar tissue. I looked like a monster, as if my face had hit every single rock on my way down the hill. God was truly after me. The message was clear: beauty is fleeting, and if my vanity was all I had, who was I now? Look how fast it can be taken away. If outer beauty is your god, what can it do for you now? Today I have come to understand, there was purpose in *every* trial and hardship the Lord has brought me through. God is intentional; He has a plan for my life. An older cousin told me, after I became an adult, that during some family gatherings when I was age seven, if there were conflicts among the children, I was good at addressing the problem. I would set everyone on what I called a peace rug and counsel those involved until a resolution to the conflict was reached. It is my testimony of God in my life, and it is not just for me; it's power for the course, preparing me to use my gift for His kingdom. A favorite scripture of mine says, in Isaiah 61:1 and Luke 4:18–19, "He came to set the captives free." John 10:10 says, "That He came to bring life and life more abundant." *Abundant* means more than enough for me and enough for sharing with others. As God comforted me through trials and tribulations, I can comfort others. He had a plan for my life. God was preparing me for change, to reflect the true lasting beauty of Gods Spirit, with new values, new beliefs, and a new perspective. He was breaking me down to build me up. He was tearing down false idols and gods, and His Word says in John 12:32, "Where He is lifted up, He will draw men to himself."

I was living hard and fast the summer of my twenty-fifth birthday. I was of the opinion that my drug abuse was in a bad state, although I did not want to see it. I was at the bottom, but not *my* bottom. I had not lost everything yet. I rationalized my drug abuse because of my mother's prescription drug abuse. When she tried to confront me on my addiction, her words were invalid. I told her she was higher than me every day. I loved her, and I knew she loved me more than anything. When she pulled that mother's-guilt card, saying that I was killing her with worry about my self-destructive lifestyle, the day she stood me in front of her full-length mirror and asked me, "Where is my child? Look at yourself. The white of your eyes are yellow, your skin is ash gray, no eyelashes, blistered lips, and burnt fingertips." By that time, I was a "chicken head," known to wear a rag on my head because my hair was uncombed. I wore three layers of clothing so that you could not tell how sucked up I was. My response to her was, "There is nothing wrong with me." I told myself I looked good; I was fine. I told her, "You get higher than me every day." I was insane. Mama wanted me to go into a rehabilitation program to get some help and because I loved her and had good health insurance from working at Ford Motors. In addition, I needed somewhere to hide from someone *very* seriously dangerous. The Mafia family I owed a lot of money for drugs. You see, at this time, my man was an old gangster-dope-dealer, a seventy-year-old married man I had pulled from a girlfriend. In my delusion, I was convinced that I was going to be rich in the drug game. This man was known in Los Angeles for doing big things in the drug world. One day he was short on the money he needed to get a kilo of pure, uncut cocaine, so I let him put up my $10,000 diamond ring as collateral for the cocaine, to be sold out of my apartment. That ring had a story of its own. An ex-boyfriend, WC, who robbed jewelry stores, gave it to me. The deal was to get my ring back in a week. He secured the property with 24-7 gunmen, surveillance cameras, and barred doors. He did not smoke cocaine, and the rule he set for me was, I would only smoke what he gave me, when he gave it to me. Just let me say that was crazy; I lost my mind and everything good about myself. I had no boundaries. No one could tell me anything. He told me the people he was doing business with were very dangerous. When they would come to the house to do business, he would send me away, trying to keep me from being seen. But I thought he was hiding money or drugs from me, so I made a point to pop in and meet Hugo. I was completely in darkness. I did not get my ring back. He had a stroke. He went into a rehabilitation hospital, and that was where I left him. I had his drugs and got smoked out. I stayed up all night, serving the drugs, carrying a long-nose, pearl-handled 25mm gun. One day, my sister Renee came to my apartment, looking for me, because I had stopped responding to calls from my family. My mind was so gone I took her into the restroom to explain what she was looking at. My apartment was a "smokehouse"; people were in all the rooms, getting high. I offered her a hit from my pipe. She looked me in the eyes and screamed out with a screeching yell, "NOOOOOOO!" and fell to her knees. Immediately the house emptied. She was devastated as she left crying, "Please stop this." Soon after, the police raided my apartment one day while I was away, and I never went back. My mother and uncle moved my things out. I moved into the jungle with another man, a brother of a friend I got high with, who had big money. Now I was living with him, who was also a smoker and selling the Mafia's drugs from his place, not really making any money, losing on deals, and spreading for parties. It was due to a loss of $360 worth of my cocaine that he hit me so hard one night upside my head—my ears rang for what seemed like hours. He had me locked in his place. I could not get past the locked bars until morning. All night he continued threatening he should kill me, so I sat still and quiet until morning. When my phone rang, I saw an opportunity. I said I had to meet my brother so he would unlock the barred door. I left with no intention of returning, not for any of my belongings.

I went to my mother, who would fight a bear for her children. She confronted him over the phone, using my brother's father's name, to get my things. I was too afraid to talk to him. Mama and the help of another male friend of mine went and got my things. I owed for the dope that was left with my dude that had the stroke and thought I could hide. Therefore, I thought the solution was leaving town, going to treatment at the Ontario Community Hospital Drug Rehab. Just a few days after entering the facility, thinking all was well, I received a call, and the voice on the other end of the phone was one I least expected. It was Hugo, the representative of the family I owed. He gave me instructions to meet with him to arrange payment. I was scared to death and did not know what to do. I called my second eldest brother, Langston, and told him my situation. I had lived with him and his angel of a wife, Janice, who was encouraging and loving throughout my addiction. This brother is the one sibling I have that was more acquainted with the drug lifestyle. He offered to take it from there, promising I would not touch it. I connected him and Hugo by phone, and that was the end of my part in that. My brother, an honorable, hardworking family man, took risk for me I can never repay. I had the nerve to be so angry with my mother for pointing out the severity of my condition, because she knew she was the only person I cared enough about to do this for. My last conversation with her, before entering the rehab program, I told her, "I am going to do this for you, and when I complete this program, I do not have anything else to say to you, and don't you say anything to me." My big brother, Langston, and his wife, Janice, drove me from Los Angeles to Ontario. On July 3, 1983, I will never forget his face, the pure shock, as we drove, and I described the lifestyle and daily activities that I had been living. With his brown eyes big and bugged, head moving from left to right, he could only utter these words: "Where was I? Why didn't I see this?"

I completed the program. While there, I received some clarity. I recognized and accepted my drug addiction. I gained the understanding that one hit is too many and there will never be enough. I cannot control it. I am an addict.

The Rules Do Not Apply
Leaves

When I first got out of rehab, I was doing well maintaining sobriety, staying away from people, places, and things that would trigger the desire to use, and surrounding myself with more healthy people, abstaining from personally drinking and drugs. It was not as hard as I thought in the beginning. I lasted as long as I could, about eight months. I seemed to be drawn to the rituals involved with smoking the pipe. I thought I could still sell drugs and be around the people, places, and things and remain sober.

One night, I proved my theory, selling at a dope house. However, I was clean and sober, looking healthy, shining like a light in the dark. The police raided the place. One officer, while restraining someone standing near me, told another officer, speaking of me, "Get her." That gave me just enough time that I pulled the sack of drugs out from under a thick belt I was wearing and tossed it through the doorway in front of me. Therefore, when I was searched, I was clean. The officer told me I did not look like I belonged there and I was told to leave. I asked the officer if I could get my shoes; they were in the bedroom. He replied, "What are you doing here? You do not belong here!" All I could think was how my family would feel about me being arrested for drugs after I had just

completed treatment. How disappointed they would be in me once again.

Just weeks following, there was a big party in Hollywood Hills hosted by Barnum and Bailey and Ringling Brothers Circus. I was there, looking good, like I was going to make it out of that rut, dressed in an all-white pantsuit fitting me fabulously, flowing and gently resting against my curves. I was having a good time, dancing on the fabulous, dimly lit patio overlooking Hollywood Hills. A man standing next to me struck up a conversation and made the comment, "Lady, you are amazing. You should be on television." I did not take him seriously; I thought he was trying to rap, but we talked a while longer. He gave me his card and said that if I called him, he believed it could happen. Upon calling the number, I discovered it to be a casting agency looking to fill an upcoming role at Universal Studios for the weekly sitcom *Diff'rent Strokes*. They asked me to come in and audition for the show. To my disbelief, I got the role. Later, I was told that 135 trained actresses from across the nation read for that part, but I got it. It was a starring role. I believed that the timing was so significant, with me needing a new start and motivation to stay sober. God knew that would bring the encouragement my life needed at that time. That was motivation for my recovery. I received so much positive attention and notoriety from talent scouts, other actors, family members, and friends. I was being recognized everywhere by fans of the show as my character, Mrs. Z. I also read for and got three smaller parts during the same time, in a matter of three months. My mom and the rest of my family were so proud. But all the while, in the back of my mind, a little voice kept saying, "They do not know me. If they knew I'm just a crackhead..." Standing at the threshold of a great opportunity many had worked hard and longed to gain, I kept looking back. I did not believe in myself, that I could really change or deserved this. I maintained sobriety and got the acting parts, one *Movie of the Week*, and another weekly sitcom. I maintained my sobriety until I received the check about four months later. Then I went back to those old people, places, and things and got high. That relapse went on for the next five years, on and off, in and out. I now believe the Word of God is true, and the scripture that says, "As a man thinks in his heart, so he is" (Prov. 23:7).

I believe, when the monster is within you, there is no threat from the outside. What you choose to believe is what you will act on. This was a perfect example of how feeling inadequate and unlovable produced thoughts of self-doubt and fear, which produced self-destructive behaviors.

Bobby

God's Plans Won't Be Stopped

After that summer, with me still in relapse, keeping company with old people and places, my cousin that I introduced to the pipe to get her off PCP years earlier introduced me to Bobby, the brother of a guy she was seeing. At first sight, he was not my type at all. Although he was tall, with an amazing body, smooth, beautiful golden-brown skin, and very big feet, he was a very nice person but lame, one of those good guys, too good for me, of the nerd type. He was a teacher, teaching at a private Christian school. He had a master's degree in mathematics from Claremont Men's College. He was a preacher's son and was actively involved in the ministry, teaching in his church. Five years previously widowed, father of one son. His hobby was flying small planes, and he was very good at playing many musical instruments. He lived with and cared for his mom in a dysfunctional household with two drug-addicted brothers. He dressed very plain, with greasy hair slicked back and the biggest goofy smile, always grinning from ear to ear. He showed no interest in material passions. He was friendly with everyone. He would help wherever he saw a need. Known wherever he went as a good person. But he was just not my type. He immediately showed he was attracted to me and began asking me out. It was some weeks later before I accepted. My intentions were not honorable, but self-serving. He knew what I was about and joked at me, calling me Satan's daughter, but he wanted me.

After we had sex, my entire view on him changed. He was an exceptional person. I loved him and needed him, more than I was aware. He had my complete heart. He loved me, took care of me, honored me, and made me want to be a better person. All he wanted from me was to stay with him and attend church. That was not a problem for me. I believed Jesus Christ is the Savior of the world, the only begotten Son of God, so attending church was not a problem. But his church was the Church of Christ, and it had some differences I do not believe were scriptural. We went, anyway, faithfully as a family. I moved in with him, and he took good care of me. Again, I could see God and His timing, and I realized how much I needed Bobby and Robert, his son, now my first child, in my life. What I did not know but learned later was that Bobby had a criminal record and substance abuse problems of his own. He told me he had a history with alcohol, PCP, and marijuana, his drugs of choice. One day, while he was under the influence of PCP, the police were called, and he was arrested for resisting arrest. The police reported he struck one of the officers. I have come to recognize that the sick attracts the sick. Bobby's drug abuse came out around the time of death of his wife five years prior. His little boy, Robert, was in the car with his mother when she died in that fatal traffic accident. Robert was injured, as he was severely cut through his mouth and jaw. Bobby worked daily and was a good provider and loved Robert and me. I had stopped smoking crack cocaine but was still smoking weed and drinking alcohol recreationally. Sick with it, still pleasing myself, running my own program.

A baby—it was all I'd ever wanted. I got pregnant, and we were extremely happy. My sister Vaughn moved in with us. His mother, whom we called Madear, was a great cook and was the most lovable, sweetest person ever, most caring family enabler who loved unconditionally. Bobby went to prison on the case while I was pregnant, and I started smoking crack again. He left me with an income of one thousand dollars a month to take care of our needs. I smoked up until I delivered my son, Shawn. My drug abuse probably caused Shawn to have cerebral palsy, although he was not diagnosed until he was around eighteen months old. I had a high-risk pregnancy with toxemia, protein in my urine, and high blood pressure. On August 9, after a routine weekly appointment, the doctor admitted me in the hospital to induce my labor because the baby was in distress. I stayed in the hospital twelve days, induced several times, until Shawn was delivered. Due to so many times being induced, Shawn suffered a lack of oxygen to his brain. Later, an attorney told me that the hospital should have performed a C-section; I could have filed a lawsuit. Honestly, I felt responsible for my son's condition. I brought Shawn home, and he seemed fine. Everything was perfect. I stopped smoking until Bobby came home, enjoying my baby boy, being a mother, and taking care of the baby I had always wanted. When Shawn was six months old, I went sneaking around with old people, places, and behaviors. I relapsed. Not once, but twice. Very soon after Shawn, we got pregnant with our second child and moved out of the house where Bobby's mother lived, into our own place. I had been one of those people that when I saw a mother with children that were stairsteps, my mom used to call them (very close in age), I would question why they would put that stress on themselves as well as deny the child the time they deserved to be the only baby. As I became that mother, I knew the answer: love.

Our beautiful daughter, Shannon, was born fourteen months later, while I was actively involved in my addiction. Because of the possibility of drug interaction, I disclosed my active drug use to the doctor during the admission process, who reported me to Child Protective Services. A social worker came to the hospital after delivery and threatened to take my baby. If it were not for Bobby being there, representing a positive support system, willing and able to care for the children, I would have needed to tell my family and find someone to release the baby to, because they would not release her to me. But God is good! My first look into her eyes, I felt so convicted. It was as if she were saying, "Please don't hurt me." It was my son Shawn's doctor that spoke up on my behalf. He said that I was a caring mother that kept my child looking cared for and kept all his scheduled appointments. It was on his word, and my agreeing, that we would meet a social worker at the house to assess my other two children and the condition of our home. I was ashamed as I waited at the house without my baby, hoping to avoid telling anyone I was not permitted to bring her home. The social worker assessed everything being decent and in order, and I went back to the hospital that same night to get my baby girl. I was so happy I was able to bring her home, so I did not have to tell my family that I was still involved in my addiction; therefore, my secret was safe. I was overfamiliar with darkness, guilt, and shame, as it was my way of life. Because CPS had been notified, they opened a case on me. I was required to attend twelve-step meeting daily and continue to test negative.

When Shawn was eighteen months old, he got sick with an ear infection. He had a high fever and was unable to sit up or walk; he was lethargic. It was a frightening time. We took him to the hospital, where he was admitted. After the doctors ran some tests, Shawn was diagnosed with cerebral palsy.

Around this time, because of the experience I had with drugs, I noticed some similarities, and Bobby's behavior began changing. He started locking the bathroom door when he used it. One particular day, I decided to search around and found residue of powder cocaine on the lid on the back of the toilet. After confronting him, I told him I could show him how to make it better. He agreed after setting his own set of guidelines and conditions in regard to how and when we would use. I really did not care about his rules or regulations; I had no intention of following them. The only thing I heard was "Okay." I showed him how to rock it up, and we started smoking it together. Our drug abuse behaviors got worse and worse very quickly. I, being an experienced smoker of ten years, with a tolerance, was able to pause and conduct myself somewhat functional. Bobby, being a new smoker, was unable to stop. There was no accountability for us. I turned my man into a crackhead, and he was stuck. Stuck in my addiction, we continued to use.

As Shannon matured, it was evident that Shawn was delayed in his development. He had a hard time balancing when he walked, and he walked on his toes. So he wore braces. He also was mentally slow, behind in his chronological age. It took a lot to care for three children. Two babies, one with special needs. It was a lot for someone like me, so self-centered, self-pleasing, spoiled, selfish, and addicted. But God was at work within me. I could not see it then, but the salvation of the Lord was at work. God never misses His aims or goals, even though there are divine delays and detours. Shawn's condition forced me to start praying daily. His needs kept me on my knees. He was my anchor to the Lord. God got bigger and bigger in my life. As I prayed, He answered daily. I wanted to be a good parent. I know now that I was not. Bobby provided well for our family. I kept the kids clean, the house clean, plenty of food in the refrigerator, and meals cooked, but my efforts were to deceive others and myself on how severe my addiction was. Everything I did was not because I loved my children but to keep CPS out of our home and keep my secret. We attended church twice weekly, all family gatherings, and even had family come to our house. Nevertheless, the truth was, neglect and abuse due to our active drug addiction continually got worse. Not once, not twice, but three times. I was the lowest of the low. The sickest of the sick.

Two years after Shannon was born, I found out I was pregnant with our third child. How interesting that my two best friends, JJ, LW, and I, all had sons born on the same date, different years. I was the last to have children among the three of us. I told Bobby, smoking so much, I was afraid the baby would have a health condition or birth defects. He said, "I trust God that He won't give us a child He is not going to care and provide for." I would get so mad when he put God in our ungodly conduct. Admitting once again that I must be the most retarded and selfish person on the planet, the lowest and the sickest of women, who had a good, caring mother with a good upbringing and good example of wom-anhood. How could I, not once, not twice, but three times, conceive and use until giving birth? My beautiful, healthy big boy, Stephen, was born ten pounds, nine ounces, and twenty-four inches long. After Stephen, I tried to get help for my addiction. I went to some outpatient counseling groups and twelve-step meetings. I did not stop using, but I did not use as much. By now, Bobby was in his own battle. He was using without me. We were growing apart because of it. He admitted how bad his addiction was and that he was losing control. He stated to me one day that he knew God would not let this go on much longer.

Bobby died January 13, 1988. Stephen was nine months, Shannon was two, and Shawn was three. It was on Robert's thirteenth birthday that Bobby died, and ten days before my thirtieth birthday. It was our usual daily routine to use; we tried to keep it a secret because Robert was old enough to know that drugs were causing a problem. We tried to hide our smoking by locking up in the room, behind locked doors, in the bathroom, while the children were watching TV or while the children were outside, playing. Or while Robert and Shawn went to school. We were not fooling anyone but ourselves. Still, we tried and failed daily. Feeling shame, guilt, and regret did not stop us. The week Bobby died was a special week, because of Robert's thirteenth birthday. We did not want to make a mess of that, in the same way we had Christmas and had to face more shame, guilt, and regret. I kept reminding Bobby that we needed to stop by making him aware of how much money we had spent and it was getting late and we needed to go to bed so that we would be able to give Robert the attention he deserved on his birthday. I thought I had convinced him to stop smoking for that night. There was once a time that he would do anything to please me. However, not at that time. And I was hurt, was angry, and felt so helpless. I did not matter to him at all. I went to bed, and shortly after, he lay down too. Nevertheless, he did not lie for long. He got up and put his clothes on while I pleaded, "Do not go." He said, "I will be right back," and left out of the house.

The Darkness before the Light

How much more negative consequences could I stand?

About an hour later, the phone rang. It was his friend who lived at Bobby's mother's house. He said, "Sheron, is Bobby there?"

I answered, "Bobby is at your house. And tell him to get home."

Joe said, "Listen, the police were at the door, talking to Bobby's brother, and I overheard them say Bobby's name and something about a fatal accident on Normandie and Imperial." He said he was going to see the accident and would call me.

It seemed like just minutes later that I saw headlights through my front window turning into my driveway. It was Joe. I opened the door. He came in, he was crying, and he said, "It's Bobby. He's dead."

I told him, "I've got to see for myself. Take me there."

I took Stephen, who was nine months old, into Rob's room and told him I would be right back. I went to the scene of the accident. We spoke very little on the way. At the scene, I saw Bobby lying there near the island of the gas station. The coroner had not arrived yet. I needed to see him for myself yet was still in disbelief that he was dead. What a hor-

SHERON CHAMBERS JEFFERSON

rible mess! My mind could not think past the present. I shut down. I was later told by Joe Bobby did go to his mother's house, where his brother smoked and sold drugs. His mother said that she saw him standing in the door of her room, and he jokingly asked, "How are you doing? Are you broke?" She responded, "I am not broke, but I am bent." That was the way they communicated, and he gave her money. She then told him to get home before he got into trouble. They found the crack he bought on him, and all the money he made that day was on him. His mom's house was a straight shot of six miles from our house. It seemed that he went and was coming right back, as he said. He stopped at a red light on Normandie and Imperial, heading west. On his left-south-west corner was a doughnut shop open twenty-four hours a day, with law enforcement in the parking lot. Unknown to Bobby, there was a high-speed police chase taking place and headed toward him at 110 miles an hour. When Bobby's light turned green, he proceeded through the intersection. The other car, driven by a nine-year-old boy and chased by the police, hit Bobby driving my car, a 1977 LTD, moving at the speed of 110 miles an hour, and forced him into the light pole, threw him out of the car 150 feet onto the island of that gas station. He died immediately from internal injury.

All I could think was, *Oh my god, what am I going to do?* Those words ran through my mind like a broken record. I returned home and paced the floor with that one thought on my mind, *What am I going to do?* until I heard another voice that said, "What can you do?" I tried searching my mind for answers, and I could find only one, stating, "Nothing, I can't do anything." I believe that was the voice of God speaking to me, my first personal encounter with God, and He said then, "Now will you let Me have your life? Would you let go and let Me have your life?" That night, I told God, "Yes.

I give up. I will let You have my life." After that unforgettable, undeniable experience with God, I remembered Robert. I went in his room and sat on the side of his bed. He sat up. I was hugging him as he asked, "What' wrong?"

My response was, "Happy birthday, Rob, but Daddy is dead."

With shock and confusion in his eyes, he asked, "What happened to him?"

As we hugged and cried, I explained, "He was killed in a car accident."

I stayed with him until he lay down to sleep, and I left the room. I made phone calls, to my mom and sister, and they came to the house. I was lost in emotions, mostly fear of what was going to happen to my children and me. I had no money. Bobby was the sole provider for us. I had nothing but my four children, a drug addiction, and a history of poor choices. Also, my thirtieth birthday was approaching. Roberts's grandmother on his mother's side had already taken Bobby to court for custody after Rob's mom died because of Bobby's substance abuse. Shortly after the funeral, Robert went to live with her. He would visit with us from time to time. I did not feel like it at that time, but it was for the best. At that time, all I could feel was more loss and sorrow. That was the second most difficult hurting, unconformable experience I had known in my life. Our families were supportive. Bobby's mother had an insurance policy that buried him. My big brother Langston and his wife, Janice, were like guardian angels; they took my babies and me and bought us whatever we needed. My cousin stepped up and took care of my babies while I prepared for the funeral. I am not sure how long she had them, but when I saw my baby Stephen, again at the funeral, he was taking steps. My mind was very foggy; I could not really think or feel anything. It was like an out-of-body experience. I appreciated my family being there to help, but I could not stand being away from my children for any amount of time. That was one of the things Bobby and I had agreed upon in raising our children: we never let them stay overnight with anyone. Another memory that stands out to me regarding the funeral is the many people who shared how positively Bobby had influenced their lives. The message of his life is, "One man did make a difference."

Bobby died ten days before my thirtieth birthday. I immediately stopped using crack after his death, putting all my attention daily toward getting through this devastation, comforting my fatherless children and the continuous flow of interacting with people. They were young and did not understand what had happened to their daddy or when he was coming back home. The three of them would stand in the front window, looking for him to pull into the drive-way as he routinely did, saying, "Dada," with that puzzled look on their face. I would hug them, cry, and tell them that Daddy was gone to be with Jesus in heaven. I do believe that God separated Bobby from his flesh to save his soul. As hard as I tried not to use and to stay away from smoking crack, it only lasted about four months. The enemy hit me with temptation every way possible. It happened regularly. Once, while running from the police, the dope man threw a bag of crack at my front door and it landed in the flower bed next to my porch. My car would seem to steer itself to the dope house when I was driving. I would stay home to sepa-rate myself from people that were involved in drugs, but they would come to my house with it and give it to me for no money. It seemed to fall from the sky. I resisted for a while, then gave in. It was worse than ever before. I did the most despicable, degrading, shameful things. Neighbors called my children "those poor babies." I repeatedly committed despicable, degrading behaviors in that time of darkness. As I tell my story, I admit to being the worst of the worst; the worst things you knew about a crackhead addict, I did. I have and will admit them to anyone who says what they will not do as an addict. I now know better than *ever* that as an addict I cannot say what I will not do. All I know is what I have not done as of yet! Based on what I have done and I never thought I would do, there is nothing I would not do for my addiction.

This went on until one day, Bobby's nephew Jackie, a very close family member, came to the house. I do not know what he saw, but what he said to me made the difference. He asked, "What are you doing to yourself? Can't you see that these kids already do not have a father and you are killing their mother? What will happen to them?" That was what motivated me to change.

My two-year-old little girl, Shannon, seemed so aware. She acted like she knew the direction of events that would take place before they happened daily, when I would go to the front door, signal the dope man over from across the street. With tears in her eyes, she would look up at me, pushing me away from the door, as if to say "No," "Don't," "You promised you would stop." As I had broken that promise so many times. Being high with no patience, having three babies, one with special needs—they only wanted to be loved and given the attention they deserved—broke my heart, and it was another influence to change. For the next nine months, this continued to build, and at the end of that year, I knew I had to make a change. The very last thing that happened was a shooting across the street from my house, and the bullet came through the window of my kids' room and penetrated their bed. The message was loud and clear: something bad was going to happen to my babies if I did not make a change.

Giving thought to what my legacy would be, when I think about the events, people, and circumstances that influenced me, it was my grandmother on my father number 2's side, Lazzetta. At the time of her death, at her funeral, I saw what a good life looks like. It was at her funeral I heard that still small voice inside again, when I thought, *I want a funeral like hers*. I heard, "You have to live life following her example." Her legacy was inspiring. To have a funeral like hers, I would need to live that kind of life. The number of people that were there seemed like thousands. Whether they were intimate and close or distant, had years of relationship, or newly introduced, they all spoke the same about her. They said she was an example of a graceful, beautiful woman of integrity, dignity, strength, hard work, wisdom, compassion, diligence, love, faith, and hope. She was not a perfect person, but she was a woman of commitment to her values." The message was that all who knew her were blessed by her life.

"The Godly walk in integrity; Blessed are their children who follow them" (Prov. 20:7). *Integrity* means righteousness, uprightness, living right with God and right with man, with complete truth and honesty.

Up until then, the way I lived would have left a legacy that was something like, "What a wasted life. She was beautiful and sweet, with so much potential. The children were rescued from her. I hope the harm she caused them won't be irreversible. She got what she wanted and would not accept the help that was offered her. It is so sad she died alone in a vacant house, a Jane Doe for weeks. The AIDS/HIV was killing her, anyway. Her poor mother's heart is broken. There will not be a funeral."

December 30, 1988, the end of the year Bobby died, God moved me out of my Egypt, Los Angeles. The house Bobby, the children, and I lived in belonged to my brother-in-law Dwight, my sister Renee's husband. They were having a house built in Rancho Cucamonga. The condominium where they were living was being sold before their new house was finished. Therefore, they needed a place to stay until their new house was ready to move in. I thought, with my income, my kids and I would end up in The Projects. But praise the Lord that was not God's plan. So Renee found me a wonderful, big, and clean apartment, affordable, in the low-crime-rate City of Montclair, located in San Bernardino County, California, and moved me in so that they could move in to the house in which I had been residing. The plan was for this to happen after Christmas. I moved out of Los Angeles December 30, 1988. I prayed from the time of Bobby's death, "Lord, if you move me from this life of addiction, give me one more chance. I will never touch it again. You will never have to hear from me about drugs again."

Although Los Angeles is my birthplace, and even though it is familiar and comfortable, it was not good for me. It was my Egypt. Where my bondage took place and I did so much evil. It was a rut for me. I describe a *rut* as a hole that one creates by walking the same familiar path back and forth every day until the path walked creates a hole. This rut, also called a hole, can be described as a grave that I dug myself so deep that my perspective is blocked and I will die there. My rut was most comfortable because of its being so familiar, where I felt a sense of control. In my rut I had lost true perspective of what was good and what was bad. My rut was so deep it was taking on the shape of the casket that I would die in. It was a dangerous place to raise my children, with drug dealers and gang members. Where nightly police and helicopters would be in my yard, where someone was hiding. My children and I would lie on the floor because of fear of bullets flying. Underneath my front porch, local dealers were hiding drugs. A young man even lay shot and bleeding once on my back porch. Bullets came through the window and landed in the children's bed. It was time for a change. I would ask myself, What was I waiting for? For something tragic to happen here, with bullets flying and my children in danger of being shot for simply wearing the wrong color?

Pruned

Something Has to Die to Bring Life

It was December 30, 1988. Bright and early that morning, my brothers and sisters came with a U-Haul truck to move my children and me to Montclair, California. I had smoked all night and was of no help in packing and moving. That next day was the beginning of my new life.

In John 14:6, Jesus said He is the Way, the Truth, and the Life. Looking back on January 13, 1988, at the time of Bobby's death, when I said yes to the Lord, life was manifesting. I believe Bobby's death brought true life to him as a believing, blood-bought child of God, and also to his children and me. Can you see where the title of this book comes from, *Thorns on the Rose*? Keep reading. The awareness of God's presence is just beginning, how He transforms trials into blessings.

Mark 9:43 tells us, if your eye, foot, or hand causes you to sin, cut it off, pluck it out. It is better to enter life lame than to be cast into hell whole. I believe The Lord separated Bobby's body from his spirit to save his soul.

Twelve months later, my heart and knees where bowed down to Christ Jesus as my Lord. Prior to that, I had received Him as my Savior, but now Lord and Savior. I now had a new passion to know God and His Will for my life. I started showing that I loved Him by learning His Word. I knew for sure that the life I had lived was insane, nothing good, darkness, all flesh, all me, and there were no good thoughts within myself, so I started reading the Bible daily with a passion for the Truth of the Gospel in all forms. I sought godly counsel and listened for the voice of the Holy Spirit to speak to me, and I did what I understood. I was sure about one thing, and that was that I do not know. Everything that I had been doing was evident of my insanity; I needed help with every thought and making every choice from someone that knew better than myself. Therefore, I did not rely on my own thinking. I asked Janice and Langston, Renee and Dwight, my mother, or Gerald and Debra—those that were doing life like I desired—for help and took the help they gave. What I now know is that people do not change until the pain of staying the same is greater than the pain of change. I could not remain the same. There was too much pain. So much pain there was no high enough to distract me from the pain I felt. Previously, I told you I did not want to stop living as I was; I did not want to change. I thought that was who I was and wanted to be. I thought I wasn't hurting anybody. *Leave me alone to enjoy my life.* My truth was, I was so afraid. Afraid that I was not smart or as good as "normal" people, and if I changed, came out of my dark environment, I would stand out as a failure. Using and abusing people, places, and things, I could not find comfort in anymore. So as fearful as change was, I had all the motivation I needed. I could no longer stand myself. Can you imagine hating everything about you? I hated being in my own skin to the point that

I avoided having a mirror and taking pictures for years. My mother mentioned to me once while visiting my home, as she had many times come, checking on me and the children in my addiction, that she had never seen a woman live without any mirrors. Bless her soul, she would even take the bus to unsafe, drug-infested areas because she loved us so. It was more apparent that during Stephen's infancy through toddler years, we took very few family and daily pictures. I am so sorry to him for what he went through, and my other children also. To make amends, I will change my life and pray that God will reward them with an abundance of blessings for their wounds.

> "Look to God for your needs, believe in Him, He is the rewarded of those who wholeheartedly seek Him" (Heb. 11:6).

I have come to understand that hurt and pain were the number one reason for substance abuse, and looking from ages ten to thirty years old at the pain I was carrying alone and trying to cover up, I know everything stems from something, a cause and effect, action and reactions. As a little girl born into my family with five older siblings, one sister just thirteen months older, who didn't live with us, I did not understand why the first four siblings had the same father and the remaining three of us each had different fathers. I believe dynamics of my personality were developed being the baby of the family when my dad was in the home. I felt loved, and it seemed I received lots of attention. That time was short-lived, and Dad was gone. I was no longer special. My happy days were few, and everything changed. My mom met my little brother's father, and he was born two years after my father left. I felt abandoned by my dad. I thought he loved me, and I did not understand how he could leave me if he really loved me, so I believed I must not be lovable. I did not realize it at that time, how those negative feelings and wounds created negative thoughts that took root and directed my behavior and actions to get that time in my life back because it was when I felt most satisfied, happy.

I can look back and see how I built my life around feelings as if they were truths, later coming to the understanding that you cannot rely on feelings because they change and the only truth is the Word of God. Remembering when I was in kindergarten, coming from school and returning to an empty house. Left alone, I went and stayed at my neighbors' house until my mom picked me up. I remember the feelings of fear, confusion, and sadness, with thoughts that they had forgotten about me and left me, assuming they no longer loved me and that must be my fault. That turned into "I will do whatever I can to assure I never feel this again." I lost my identity in people-pleasing. The effects these events had on my thoughts and behaviors turned me into a people-pleaser, with thoughts that I would work hard to do and say all the right things to be loved and accepted by others. I worked so hard not to feel that hurt of not being good enough for people to love that I did not know who I was. I became whoever and whatever I thought others wanted. I was so fragile that I could not accept being confronted with my imperfections. My being confronted with a human error or mistake caused me to act out in an aggressive, defensive manner rather than admit I was wrong or had made a mistake. The issue was inadequacy. Being raised by a single mom with seven children and an illness and prescription medication abuse and emotional abandonment, being in poverty and on welfare, and being different from all my peers because of my size— that's a pattern that screams insecure! I have no doubt Mom gave all she had, and I know Mom went above and beyond to provide and create a clean, safe place to raise her seven children. Mom was a disciplinarian with strong family values. She valued her children as well her image. Growing in size rapidly, I was always known as the big girl, the tallest in my class. At nine years old, I was already five feet, nine inches tall, and by the age of twelve, I had reached six feet tall. I reached six feet, six inches tall, and that was the last time I cared to measure my height. My unusual size had a lot to do with my feeling inadequate. I did not fit in. Constantly feeling hurt and rejection, being ridiculed by cruel people. Because of my mother's illness, I felt sadness and fear consistently, believing she was going to die and I would not have know one who really loved me or that I could love with all my heart.

But God, He had a plan for me. Me, a hopeless dope fiend, transformed into a dopeless hope fiend. The first scriptures I claimed and stood on, given to me by my big sister: "Whosoever calls on the name of the Lord shall be saved" (Rom. 10:13).

> "God who forgives all your iniquities, who heals all your diseases' who redeems your life from destruction, who crowns you with loving kindness and tender mercies" (Ps. 103:3–4).

> "The Lord restores my soul; He leads me in the path of righteousness For His Name's sake" (Ps. 23:3).

God's grace and mercy had saved me, picked me up out of the miry clay, kept my children and me, and brought us from death to life. God put His bright love light on my darkness and showed me who and what I am apart from Him. God gave me new hope and identity in Christ Jesus.

The significance of the year 1988 and every event, situation, and circumstance, God, if not in His Perfect Will, then in His Permissive Will, allowed to be accumulated. He was building up the irrefutable evidence that I need God the Father, the Son, and the Holy Spirit, the fullness of It. He knows me, and He knew what I needed in order to change. That year, He set me on the path of Life. God was my only Hope. I had tried everything else, everything within my power, and failed. I searched for fulfillment, peace, contentment, purpose, and significance and could not find it until I surrendered to the Lord Jesus.

January 13, 1988, even though it was not visible to the carnal eye until the following year, I was in the process of Spiritual growth. This was like I once planted roses and the bush seemed like it was dying, not flourishing, and would not live the first season. However, the following season, it came to life and started producing stems, then thorns, then green leaves and buds, and then eventually, roses.

The first morning of my new life, December 31, 1988, I knew everything had changed, was different, unfamiliar, good, and fresh, in all aspects, mentally, physically, and spiritually. It seemed as if the atmosphere shifted. I could now see what I was not long ago able to see. I was more aware of the beauty around me and the contrast of how dark and chaotic it had been in my life. Yet still in what seemed like a fog, processing hurt, the grief and loss of Bobby, anger, denial, blame, and bargaining, and all I wanted was to get over it, put it behind me. There is a saying that time heals all wounds. That is not truth. The truth is, wounds left unaddressed feaster. Decay sets in, and it gets worse, does not heal. Even if it scabs over, it leaves ugly scars. That becomes what we call in life baggage, clutter, strongholds, habits, and hang-ups, which block the path of our future. Also, processing the move to an unfamiliar place, away from everyone I know, learning to make new choices, overcoming drug addiction, grief, and loss, habitually thinking errors of being alone with God and my three small children, now two years old, three years and five months old, and four years two months old, was a challenge. Traditionally, to celebrate Roberts's birthday, which was the anniversary of Bobby's passing, we went back to Los Angeles. We would bring Rob gifts, spend time with him, and visit Bobby's family so that the kids would know them and they would know how we were doing. My total focus was raising my children to be decent and godly, being the mother I wanted to be, giving all that I had. I knew Bobby would have been pleased; this was how he wanted life for his family. He had an abundance of spiritual knowledge and influences that, at that time, I was not able to understand.

First Corinthians 13:11 says we become adult when we put away childish ways. It took me a long time to get any understanding, experiencing many lessons through trials and tribulations, more than most would need. The under-standing of stewardship was one of the first God gave me. As a steward, I was accountable and responsible to God for everything He had given me. Especially the souls of these children He has entrusted to me. They are His, on loan to me. God allowed their father to be removed and left them in my care because He has a plan for them, for good and not for harm. This privilege to train them up in the admiration of the Lord was given to me, to train them in the way that they should go, and one day I will stand before the Lord to give an account for what I did and did not do with what He gave me. I knew without a doubt that I had made such a mess with my past. This was my opportunity to get it right, make amends before God, repent. That became my driving force. First, please God and raise my children.

In James 1:12, God promises, "Blessed is the man who preservers under trials, passed the test." I was now living for the day when I'd stand before the Lord to receive that Crown of Life. But God, that would have been my legacy. Still a long journey to travel, I was hopeful. Now that Jesus was my Lord, something in me had changed. I did not need drugs. I would like to say my addictions were gone, but they were not. I was able to say no to drugs, though I still struggled with other habitual behaviors, addictions to pleasing my flesh using sex and materialism. I knew it was an addiction because it controlled me. I used sex and indulged in it, knowing it was a sin, and caused the familiar feelings of guilt and shame. Like drugs, it temporarily masked reality, brought on negative feelings of guilt, of regret, and cost me too much. Nevertheless, I would not stop. I was sexually promiscuous, immoral, a sinner before the Lord. I felt worse as I continued because of my relationship with Jesus, being Saved and Born Again. Through this, I learned a valuable lesson, to watch out for those secret sins. I found that they were attached to my strongholds. Many of my regrets and shame were attached to my sexual sins. There was no limit to what I would do in trying to fill the emptiness. In reality, that behavior was disobedience, pleasing myself, that hindered the work of the Holy Spirit and hurt my Lord. Praise God, the Vine gives life. God is the Gardener.

"I am the true grapevine, and my Father is the gardener" (John 15:1). God the Father meets each of us where we are individually using what's familiar to us, pictures, things, places, and people, and that's where *Thorns on the Rose* was birthed, through the picture of His relationship with people. The Living Lord Jesus's Life-giving Power at work in us creates beauty. Like a gardener working hard, He gains great joy caring for the vineyard, yielding a crop. Like a hardworking gardener, He does everything possible to ensure a good and abundant harvest.

Remove the Weeds

Cannot Mix the Old with the New

I made the mistake of mixing my new life with my old life only to prove you should not bring your past into the future. Let the past go once you have learned from it. In Genesis 19:26, Lot's wife looked back at Sodom. In 1 Samuel 15, God told Saul to destroy everything. In Luke 9:62, Jesus said to him, "No one who puts his hand to the plow and looks back is fit for the kingdom." Second Corinthians 5:17 says there should be no looking back. Live as a new creation.

Three years into my new life walking with the Lord, I ran into a boyfriend from my past. He was the guy my cousins introduced me to from the East Side after my breakup with Little Daddy. It was this person that gave me my first up close and personal experience with a crackhead, and that was why our relationship ended. It was a bad breakup. Three years later, with three young children and in my third year of transformation, abstinence, and improvement in many ways, with yet a long way to go, while I was visiting Los Angeles, our paths crossed again. We exchanged contact numbers and began communicating weekly. He admitted to his drug problem and many offenses and asked if I would forgive him. I told him my story. WC shared that since we last saw each other, he had been incarcerated at a state rehabilitation prison. There he had received a drug treatment program, where he learned a lot about himself and his disease of addiction. He committed to never using again. Blah, blah, blah. Remember, I told you I am one of God's most retarded daughters, and after six weeks, with my sick self, we began sleeping together. He would ride the bus out to my house in Montclair. At first, on an overnight, then weekends. He ended up moving in. I hoped we were walking the same path of change and growth, but he was not. He was not using, but he was still using the same old thinking and showing his character flaws. He was just abstinent.

He was still robbing from jewelry stores, making lots of money, but my attraction was still great sex. I also was still in need of a change of character. This habitual thinking error was connected to my poor self-image and the unhealthy behaviors I had adopted and practiced for many years to create a sense of comfort with relationships. The point to me sharing this behavior is that I have many regrets, but this was my biggest. As character flaws go, the most important character is integrity; either you are a person with integrity, all or not at all. He admitted that he had stolen my gold rope chain with the eagle charm, the one I had accused my sister of stealing. I chose to make an allowance for that and forgive, understanding that was the disease of addiction, and to please the lust of my flesh, which was my addiction.

Then, you see, one day, my little girl, Shannon, was sitting on his lap as we sat having a conversation, and he touched her between the legs. I noticed when she got down and left the room she had a certain look on her face. She went to her room, and I followed her there, and she told me what he had done to her. I didn't want to believe it! I questioned her for details and told her I would take care of it. I wanted to make it go away! She and I went back to confront him. He acted surprised and swore he had never intentionally touched her. He said maybe he accidentally touched her and apologized to Shannon. After that, I told Shannon, "From now on, we will no longer sit in any men's lap." I hoped that was the end of it. However, a month later, it devastated me when he slept with one of my best friends, and that was the end! I had always had her on a pedestal, had even been jealous of this friend. She seemed to have everything I didn't. She had an alluring look that attracted men. To give it a name, I would use the word *sexy*, and she wore it well. Her style of clothes revealing all her sexiness, long weaved hair, and her pedicure and manicure weekly. I wanted to be like her. She had a good job with the school board of education. I guess she thought that she was supposed to have everything I had. She chose to disrespect our relationship for a chance at a big diamond ring too. I believe this saying: "Show me your friends and I will tell you who you are." I forgave her, although she denied it repeatedly. I was hurt to my core. I believed him. He admitted and told me when their plan started, and all the details. He told me she was jealous of me and what I had. It shattered me and almost broke me. I was down for a while, but I got back up again. I blamed him, but I had a part to play in it and chose to take responsibility.

I will never put another person on a pedestal or give trust to a person that lacks integrity. I had given my life to the Lord, and my desire was to walk upright. I had a lot of compromise in my life that needed to be removed, even more than I was aware of. Sex was a problem, but it was more than sex; it was deeper, lust of the eye, lust of the flesh, and the pride of life, as told in 1 John 2:16–17. I was more about pleasing myself, no matter what it cost. Selfishness, self-pleasing, self-centeredness, without boundaries, with no self-discipline.

Just a few months following WC, while getting over the devastating hurt of being deceived by someone I considered a best friend since childhood, I was still taking on more self-inflicted wounds, hurt, grief, and loss, to address them. I did what I was learning to do when overwhelming life issues showed up. I committed myself to spending quality time with Jesus. I call it going to the top of the mountain with Jesus, to remove all distractions and sit at His feet. I would share the Word I received with my children and whomever I could, to encourage. I shared my testimony every opportunity I had. I had all the children involved in Little League Baseball and spent Saturdays at the park and Sundays at church. Life was simple and good.

God Did Not Intend for Us to Walk This Journey Alone

Growing Clusters

The time came when it seemed like there were people that had less than me and needed what I had been blessed with. The people God placed in my life, like SV, a young woman God sent into my life who became my roommate and friend. She was a few years younger than me and had recently moved to the United States from Jamaica with dreams of making a life for herself and her daughter. She left her daughter with her parents in Jamaica. I had little, but I had all that I needed, which was more than enough, and some to share when the Lord supplied. She was Godsent. We needed each other. She was help with the kids and the God-seeking, accountability friend I needed. I received a lesson from her I won't forget. After WC, about five months later, I met another guy, named Darwin, and we started dating. He was generous with his money, great with the kids. They really liked him because he was a lot of fun; he kept us active, going places and always doing fun things together as a family. Of course, he and I were frequently sexually active.

Again, old sinful behaviors ruling my life. I was trying to fit old wine in a new wineskin (Luke 5:36–39). Bringing old behaviors into my new life. One day, after Darwin had spent the night, SV, my roommate and friend, who was also beginning her walk with the Lord, and I had a conversation on forgiveness of sins. She pointed out the fact that I was sinning, sex outside of marriage. I pointed out that it was sin having sex but I prayed for forgiveness. I read the scripture that says God forgives more than man, seventy times seven. I know now that I was really twisting and manipulating the Word to fit the way I wanted it to. SV replied firmly, asking, "What Bible are you reading? You didn't read the part where it says, 'Confess and repent, turn away from your sins, and He will cleanse and forgive your sin.'" Praise God for friends like her, for confronting sin and pointing me to the truth and away from deception.

I had met Darwin when I started working at Kmart in October for the holiday season. I was looking forward to giving my children a good Christmas. My only income had been receiving welfare. It was there that I met Darwin standing a few cashiers from mine, watching me and trying not to be seen, avoiding eye contact. He was with a woman, but that didn't matter, because he was so fine. He was tall, rich brown skin, with big beautiful brown eyes and an awesome physique—just my kind. I didn't know it at that time, but he had just gotten out of prison. Go ahead! It's okay to laugh at how repeatedly stupid I was. We eventually got married and remained so ten years, all of them he was in prison. I met him the day after he was released from prison, having served almost thirteen years. At that time, I was in my third year of transformation, a thirty-three-year-old mother of three young children. Widowed after the death of Bobby and starting life in a new place. All I had was Jesus, and my focus was to get close to Him.

I remember it was my thirty-third birthday. Although there was a celebration with friends and family, I was still sad. When I talked to my big sister about how I felt, about being so far behind in life with nothing to show, she stopped me and said there was plenty to be thankful for. For one thing, I was sober and in my right mind; I had all my babies, and they were healthy. I didn't get them taken away. As I reflected on what she said, her perspective, my sorrow changed to gratitude and joy. As I continued to think with that perspective on how much I had come through and how only God made it possible for me and my children to have what we had and be where we were, I maintained we were blessed.

I was just mothering my kids, working at Kmart to increase my income. I was a cashier. When I saw Darwin, both our heads were above everyone else's; he was as tall as me, shining like new money. We had a moment of eye contact and looked away quickly. The woman he was with was his mother, unbeknownst to me at that time. She was directing his attention toward me. That day was my last day working at Kmart. My mindset was still on the low road. I did not want to work for the same monthly income I could sit home and get on welfare check. So I quit. I went home that day and told my friend and roommate, SV, about this fine man at work that looked like black Jesus and seemed to be attracted to me. Two weeks later, I saw him again in the market. As I walked toward the direction where he was shopping, I attempted to pass him. He grabbed my shopping cart and introduced himself, reminding me of the day he saw me at Kmart. He told me he had gone back since then, inquiring about me, and was told I no longer worked there. Trying to hold back my smile, I said, "It was good meeting you.

Maybe I'll see you around." Then attempted to walk away. He grabbed my shopping cart and said, "Wait, I told myself if I saw you again, I would never let you go." He asked if we could exchange numbers, so we did. Before I reached home, my roommate told me he had called already. We connected right away, enjoyed each other's company. He was great with my kids. He always came with gifts and was very generous financially.

I got pregnant right away. He got spooked, and he stepped back from the relationship the first few months. So soon after being released from prison and serving thirteen years, this degree of a relationship was overwhelming for him. After counsel from his mom, grandmother, and two sisters, when he came back, we were happy again and stayed together, but he never moved out of his sister's place or committed completely to our relationship. His drinking was the biggest problem for me. I was insecure, jealous, controlling, and full of fear and was on a mission to get as far away as possible from any hurtful, dysfunctional behaviors, especially those I was already overfamiliar with. Still, I continued to be disobedient. Although I knew better. My sexual behavior continued. Other areas that I needed to work on were my cursing and the way I yelled at my children, which was verbally abusive. I could rationalize and justify my behavior and say it was learned behavior from my mother, or I could say I was overwhelmed being a single mom in early stages of my recovery, but there is no justification. I was wrong. I needed to change this, as well as many other areas. I truly needed to be transformed.

Praise God He was working in me! Whether I could see Him or not. He is faithful to complete the work He started (Phil. 1:6). Unbeknownst to me—and I say that because the people from my past that were watching curiously would say,

"You are not the same. What's up with you?"—God's Word was at work in me. I was being transformed by the renewing of my mind (Rom. 12:2). New values and beliefs were changing the way I lived—new things I did and old things I no longer did. My change was slow, little by little. As I've told you, I was the Lord's most retarded child. But the Word of God says in 1 Peter 2:9, Ephesians 5:14, Matthew 6:33, and Proverbs 21:21, I am His own special people, to "awake you who sleep, arise from the dead and Christ will give you light." More than anything, desire God's righteous rule on this earth and in your life. The person who follows life, righteousness, and honor has a more abundant life. All these things are a gift from the Lord. I made a commitment to the Word of God as absolute truth in my life, and it changed my perspective, reshaped me to overcome being retarded. I surrendered my way and followed Him, to the best of my ability. Believing the Lord has a better plan for my life than I. He was preparing me to endure and overcome (Heb. 10:36; Rev. 21:7). Looking back on the process, I was a very self-centered, selfish person.

I have learned people travel different roads to find faith in God. Some have a dramatic experience with God and never doubt Him again. Others struggle with conflicting and perplexing ideas that they finally resolve. There are those that live a promiscuous and ungodly life, and only when they are on the verge of despair do they seek a better road and find it in Christ. That is my story.

Pruning
The Fire

When I was seven months pregnant, I relocated to a brand-new home in Chino. My sister-in-law Debra, who worked for Chino City Hall, helped me get the house through a rent-to-own program. The house was beautiful, perfect for me and my children. I decorated in my favorite color. Everything was new and peach—furniture, blinds, walls. Only the carpet was beige. There was a nice fenced-in yard, and the outside of the house was painted peach. The neighborhood seemed very quiet and family-oriented. We had been there only three weeks, still unpacking, and my babies' daddy did not live with us.

One night, just before putting the children to bed about nine o'clock, we were in the living room, watching television, when someone threw two Molotov cocktails, a simple bomb made from a bottle filled with gasoline and stuffed with a piece of cloth that is lit just before the bottles are thrown, in this case through the front window. Following the bombs, eight bullets, from a 9mm, whizzed through the room. Some hate-filled people came to kill us that night. People we did not know and did not know us. The police deemed it was a hate crime because the newly built house was in a section of Chino identified as the Barrio and we were the first blacks to move in on that street. We knew it was motivated by racial hate, because they spray-painted on the front of my house on the garage door the words "Death to All Niggas!" It just happened that the police department was right around the corner, so when I called 911 and the operator said, "Go out to the front of the house," I told her we were afraid to because they were shooting. She assured me there were already police there. Praise God we were not hurt, although we were traumatized, in shock. The house burned to the ground in a few short moments. God was at work, protecting us.

Scripture says, "No weapon formed against me shall prosper" (Isa. 54:17). God was also correcting me in the area of being materialistic, idolatry to "stuff money could buy," which was another stronghold. During this situation, He showed me that nothing of real value burned in that fire. Only the man-made, replaceable items, and the true items of value were the souls of my children and me, and the Lord brought us through that. I believe with my whole heart any trial/thorn in life you turn over to God, He will make you better from it. He will make something beautiful from it (rose). God has been so good to me. He abundantly increased my income. I started receiving the children's Social Security and Shawn's disability benefits. We had all brand-new furniture, in our brand-new house that I was renting to own. Still twisted with self-esteem issues, perpetrating an image of "I'm good, look what I have," I was thinking more of the gifts God had given me than of the gift-giver Himself. God let me watch my idols, little gods, burn to the ground. The still, gentle voice within me asked, "Now, who are you if you have no possessions?" That was the question I had to answer.

I had been humbled and taught a valuable lesson. I was not completely changed regarding my materialism, but I was put on the right path, and I was sure what matters and are most valuable to God are people and souls. And the possessions that God had allowed me to have, He could replace. He is unlimited. My perspective and values were changing. I heard the loving voice of my Lord God in this very trying time: 1 Peter 1:7, Job 23:10, and Zechariah 13:9. These scriptures tell us about how God, the Refiner, uses fire to separate the dirt from the gold to make it pure. I was grateful to the Lord for sending Laneisha; she immediately responded on the spot, with so much help. She was the person responsible for contacting Channel 5 News and getting me the abundance of donations. I would not have thought of that. I was seven months pregnant with her brother's child when the fire happened. What stood out differently about me was when the news reporter from Channel 5 News interviewed me. He asked me what I wanted to see happen to whoever had done this, and I replied, "The Lord is just, and He will judge." It seemed as if everyone thought I was full of anger. The truth was, I was so grateful we had not been hurt there was no room in my heart for anger. I was so grateful for our lives. The rose was beginning to form. I was seven months pregnant, and my three children and I were burned out of our home and shot at by a 9mm, eight rounds, and two Molotov cocktails were thrown through the window of our home. But we were alive, and I was grateful! Darwin became very angry and protective of us. He stayed very close by my side while we were homeless. We were living in one of his mother's vacant houses so that we could be together. My children and I could have stayed with family, but he would not have been able to be with us because we were not married. I wanted to be with him. We all stayed in one of his mother's vacant houses that had empty rooms. We all slept in the same bed together.

Rose: There are no coincidences with God. It was a blessing that the morning of the fire, I had received my accep-

SHERON CHAMBERS JEFFERSON

tance letter in the mail from the County of San Bernardino Housing Authority, stating my low-income housing application had been approved. The application was submitted two years prior. In addition, after Channel 5 News came to the burned house to interview me, they set up a fund for the children and me, and people from all over, of all ethnicities, gave truckloads in abundance of everything, including money. It was a challenge to decide what to do with so much stuff. I thought I was being humble, so I did not want to throw anything away. After watching everything I owned burn to the ground, I was thankful to have anything. I even tried to keep some of our clothes that were in the washing machine at the time of the fire and did not burn, but the smell of the smoke was overpowering in them. I had to throw them away.

My sister Renee and I had a strong disagreement concerning things. I, as the person with absolutely nothing, and I guess my faith was wavering, could not see how we would get all our needs met. So I took anything and everything, no matter the condition. But Renee, through the eyes of faith, was trying to convince me that God had better plans for me and would supply. So I let go of the burn-smelling clothes and the donated furniture that was not really to my liking. Just like she said, it happened. Almost immediately, like Renee said it would, above and beyond anything I could think or imagine (Eph. 3:20). So much that I could have furnished several houses, I gave what I did not want away. People came with nonstop donations and repeated messages, that they were sorry for the hate demonstrated against my family, that that was from a wicked few and was not the heart of the majority. The city of Chino gave me a check for $25,000 to buy new whatever we needed. We were homeless for six weeks, until we received an apartment through the housing authority.

After the fire, we were homeless for about six weeks and then moved to the Benson Street Apartment. One month later, I gave birth to DJ, a beautiful son, nine pounds, fourteen ounces, twenty-two inches long. Our beautiful, healthy baby boy Darwin Jr. was born the following December after I started dating his father. December 21, just days before Christmas. Darwin Sr. was not there for his first child's birth; he was back in jail, incarcerated again. Everything happened so fast because I was still so needy and in a hurry to fall in love, trying to fill the hole in my soul that is for God with a lesser god. We moved so fast. Let me correct that and take my responsibility: I moved too fast, using that same destructive thinking that I should have it because I want it. It was after I got pregnant that I could see his unhealthy, negative behaviors, his alcoholism, which caused problems within our relationship. He had character flaws that surfaced when he drank. It was as if he had a split personality, like my daddy number 1, Otis Chambers. He was a hardworking family guy during the week, a drunken party animal on the weekends. I also was told that many of his behaviors were like his father's. His father had a drinking problem, and he had been incarcerated twenty-five of Darwin's early years. I was so wounded, small in my own mind, with extreme feelings of inadequacy. I felt privileged to be with him.

My dear niece and friend Tracy responded to my call that evening requesting her to come stay with the children while I drove myself to the hospital. I had been told there was a boy in every bottle of castor oil, so I drank a bottle and waited for the contractions to start. I could not wait until the baby was ready to come; he was already past due date, and Christmas was approaching quickly. Coming from the life they had been subject to and experiencing the fire Shawn, Shannon, and Stephen had experienced, I was determined to give my babies the good life they deserved. I was making amends. It was just days before Christmas, after the move into our three-bedroom apartment on Benson Street in Chino, California, and a radio station was having a Christmas make-a-wish contest. I wrote in my Christmas wish for my four children and won. The prize was $2,500, and they read my letter on the radio. In it I gave thanks to the Lord for all His goodness in caring for us through the attempted murder, being shot at, burned out, homeless, and starting over in a new apartment at Christmas.

It was there on Benson Street that God placed good people, like Stella, a caring single Hispanic mom of two teen-age girls, in our lives. She was there for my children and me, sharing all that she had, an example of generous, unconditional love. Stella's name was among the first words DJ spoke. There were many people placed in my path. I could go on and on to show how God was developing the rose with these people—some were used to prune me, to cut off or trim back unwanted parts for better shape or more fruitful growth; some to fertilize, cause me to develop and make me more productive. Fertilizer smells bad because it's made of waste, but it's used for the good of the rose, some to nurture, care for, and encourage the growth or development. To care for, giving necessary attention needed for healthy development. Some to teach what not to do. People like Betty, single with one daughter and son, then adopted a baby boy. A strong woman that was independent, a go-getter, beautiful, fun-loving—a giving person and friend. She set a great example for me of what it looks like to be all a woman can be. Her home was clean and beautiful always, as well as her children, and she kept herself up stylishly dressed. She worked a job, raised her children, and made time for herself. The Murphys and her four children—three girls, one boy—single, a black family. Their mother had a twin sister and a big family that was very close. She was sick, died of cancer. The children were young; their father came to stay in the home so they could stay together. They spent a lot of time at my apartment. All these people served a purpose in my early development as a Christian. God is intentional; there was no accident. Anna was a young Hispanic woman, single mom, with two boys and two girls. She seemed shy, worked a job, trying to do her best to provide for her children, and took time to show them love, interacting in fun, games, and outings. She and I both had things in common, made evident by our choices in men. Both of our babies' daddies were stuck in addictions, serving time in prison. I could not see myself even while looking in a mirror, but looking at her, I could see myself; she was a reflection of myself. Now, at this juncture of my journey, in spite of my flaws, many shortcomings, sins, afflictions, and iniquities, the Lord God knew the plans He had for me, and I was beginning to see and believe and hope in Him and that plan. It's been said God rarely heals all the brokenness in a person's life. Even His servant Paul was told, "My grace is sufficient for you," when he sought healing for the thorn in his flesh. Nonetheless, much healing is available to those whose lives are intimately interwoven with His. Ask, and you will receive (James 4:2; 2 Cor. 12:7–9; Matt. 7:7).

I felt closer to Darwin because we shared that traumatic experience of the attack on the children and me; it bonded us together on another level. I got my children help from therapist, through Victims of Crimes, while I prayed and praised God for keeping His hedge of protection around us. Bless their little hearts, my children were traumatized. That is a lot for someone so young to process alone. I believe God would use it all for our good as a family, individually, and as an example for somebody. It's like when you take a picture, there is the main object you focus on, and there is the background. I believe the background objects are equally important to the Lord.

This truly was the hand of God over our lives (Isa. 29:11). He loved me enough to speak to me from the deepest heaven. I heard Him in the depths of my heart. Deep calls unto deep. He blessed me to allow me to hear Him so clearly. I felt so privileged. I prayed that I do not take that for granted and have a right response, a heart overflowing with gratitude.

Rose: My heavenly Father was training me to value the things of the Spirit, lasting things, those things not just good but what's best, and stay with a thankful mindset and to build my house on a firm rock, where the storms of life would not be able to shake me (Luke 6:48). As I was learning these lessons, I was to teach them to others. God was preparing the way, placing people in my path, cultivating my mind and heart, first to Him, and then for others. There was a call on my life, an anointing that I was being prepared for. I have had strangers tell me they can tell I have an anointing and ask if there are any preachers in my family. My grandmother was a pastor. The Lord is into preparation, and He had chosen me. He was making something out of nothing, as He has been known to do. First, bringing me to the end of myself, tearing me down to build me up, was what He did.

We can see God's Word in preparing, as with Joseph in the book of Genesis. Moses read Exodus, Saul the apostle, whose name was changed to Paul (Acts). The Bible confirms the preparation of many of God's chosen.

The key to the house withstanding the storm is not the external appearance; the Spirit works from the inside out (Matt. 7:24–25). The key to the house enduring is the foundation. To endure life, one must have proper relationship to

Christ, to stand the test of Christ. Without the proper relationship, you will fail the test, but it is an open-book test. First John 2:17 says the world is passing away, and the lust of it, but he who does the will of God abides forever.

A quote by Neil A. Maxwell: "God does not begin by asking us about our ability, but only about our availability, and if we then prove our dependability, He will increase our capability!"

God uses all things for His glory.

Rose: I am grateful my family was *very* supportive of me and my efforts to live right. I was given a car from my brother-in-law Dwight just before I moved out of Los Angeles. It was a stick shift. I burned the engine out, and Dwight paid for the repairs. I sold that car for $1,200. Dwight was proud of me and the way I upgraded. I purchased a car from the auction and drove it until we outgrew it and bought a brand-new Ford van. I sold my old car to SV for $700, and she drove it for four more years. I was happy about the new van, but it taught me a good lesson about getting what I want and the real cost I have to pay. I did get the car I wanted, but I was so focused on what I wanted I used no wisdom and sought no counsel. I ended up paying 25 percent over the price of the car in interest rate. I was driving a Ford at the price of a Mercedes.

ROSE: Remembering some other people placed in my life that helped me grow spiritually. When I look back, it amazes me to see how good God is at providing a way out of no way. Being clean and sober just four years, coming out of total darkness, and having people still have hope for me was a miracle. Surrendering my life to Christ, I could see God taking care of me better than I did for myself. All of God's Word is true.

"To him who has ears let him hear, and eyes, let him see" (Matt. 11:15; Rev. 2:29). His love covers a multitude of sin. My family stated as a whole and individually; they said I had given and cared for each of them at a time when they were in need and I had it coming, so they were glad they could be there for me. Because of my long history of making poor choices, with no self-value, I had to think really hard to remember any good I had done. I could not, so I just took their word. Most of my misery stems from feeling unloved. This feeling comes from abandonment issues, and the perceived feeling is often worse than the actual event itself. My fear of reliving the feeling caused all my dysfunctional behaviors. For instance, sabotaging relationships, isolating, making everything about me, being undisciplined and unorganized, and having no integrity. These behaviors made it impossible for me to ever be able to get what I really wanted out of life, and what I really wanted most was to be loved. I have found that love only comes as a gift. You can't earn it. I was learning to be willing to be vulnerable to receive the gift. Receiving a new perspective through the Word of God, I have experienced more love in my life than I deserve or could earn. It is all grace. God was pursuing me, drawing me to Himself, with His everlasting love. Still, I struggled back and forth, wanting to control my life. The dominating voice of my old nature, weak and empty as it was, yet sometimes overpowering at times, because it was what was most familiar and comfortable. It was stronger, less familiar than my new nature.

For every failure in my life—and there were many—I felt either guilt or shame, sometimes both. It's been more of my failures than my successes that have opened me up to the love of God, which has drawn me out of the darkness, thus the title of this book, *Thorns on the Roses*. These struggles taught me to go sit at the Lord's feet in prayer, praising Him with songs, and meditate on Scripture. The more I praised, prayed, and read, the more I learned about Him. His will for my life and how my choices to sin, to choose my way over His, hindered the things He has for me (John 6:33–35). I learned to be more disciplined by choosing the truth of God's Word over my feelings. I have many sins and some strongholds that look like addictions. I struggled with obedience because I lacked self-discipline and was so self-centered. That means no value for the truth, no integrity, and no love of God, which showed no God. God was not in His rightful position in my life. God was not on the throne of my life. Sin, the lust of my flesh, still reigned. Even after I said yes to the Lord, for Him to have His way with my life, and really believed that He could do better than me, I kept taking the controls back. I wanted to be like David, his desire to be like an open book, a glass-house for God to cleanse and change me. The answer to this problem was getting to know the Lord God through His only begotten Son, Jesus, and to just obey Him. It wasn't easy, but I didn't turn back, nor did I quit. Remember who I told you I am, God's most retarded daughter. God's Word is the truth, and I am a perfect example of 2 Corinthians 12:7–9, which says "My grace is sufficient for you, for my strength is made perfect in weakness. I would rather boast in my infirmities."

Rose: In spite of my strongholds, what I wanted most was love, and love is a gift. I was learning to be willingly, actively open to receive the gift. I know it is a gift, because I have experienced, since surrendering my life to Christ, more love in my life than I believe I deserved or could earn. It was all grace, God pursuing me. I had been to the bottom of the pit, and there was only one way left to go, and that was up, one day at a time. I would take three steps forward, two steps back, but I would not let go of His hand (1 Pet. 5:6; Jer. 32:17; Isa. 48:13: John 1:3).

Rose: I was changing, but it was a slow process. More change in some areas and less in others. I did come to recognize I needed structure and discipline very much for a better life, realizing that the lack of discipline and structure permitted consistent failure. One of the first, and a major, change I committed to was to no longer leave the house after dark. It was easy to recognize that a pattern for everything in my sinful life happened after dark. Therefore, anything I had to do had to be done during daylight hours. I no longer slept in late; I got up early for prayer, praising the Lord with singing and Bible reading. I started with only a verse and quiet time before waking the children. Now, with God's peace throughout the house, I would wake the children with a song to start their day, instead of anxieties; rushing and screaming at them was another change made. Another change had to do with people I would go around and those I allowed to come around me. The only people allowed shared the same values and were like-minded in making changes within themselves. I helped others with less than myself. Another change for me was sharing all that I could. What I had most was a clear understanding that my thoughts and ways had been my problem, that I should have faith in God's Word, however small—and you know what the Word says about faith the size of a mustard seed (Luke 17:5–6). Watching God do for me what I could not do for myself, time and again, with very little money, only a welfare check. But He met the needs. With more bills than money at the beginning of every month, yet at the end, not only were the needs met, but more often than not, we also received wants. My kids did not go without. With four kids, there were a lot of needs, and because of the wonderful example my mother raised me with, I wanted to give my children all their wants. God supplied over and over.

I remember the day. It was the first of the month, and I was calculating, praying, and doubting over the monthly needs when that still small voice within said, "Really, Sheron? You still don't see Me? I am here. I will provide" (Eph. 2:18). "I am all that you need! Stop worrying and learn to trust Me!" I had seen His faithfulness too often *not* to believe. I had changed in some areas, not in all, but I was learning to trust the Lord more and more.

Nonetheless, "the Lord is good and His mercy endures forever," where sin abounds grace much more, and His grace is sufficient (Ps. 100:5; Rom. 5:20; 2 Cor. 12:9). I was blessed. I've read and believe God speaks to His servants. What He said to me is, "Wait with Me for a while. I have much to tell you. You are walking along the path I have chosen for you. It is both a privileged and a perilous way, experiencing My glorious presence and heralding that reality to others. Sometimes you feel presumptuous to be carrying out such assignments. Don't worry about what other people think of you. The work I am doing in you is hidden at first, but eventually blossoms will burst forth, and abundant fruit will be borne. Stay on the path of life with Me. Trust Me wholeheartedly, letting my Spirit fill you with joy and peace" (1 Kings 8:23; Gal. 5:22–23).

Thorn: Remembering back when I wanted a baby so badly and thought I couldn't have them—how wrong I was! It was only nine months after the birth of Darwin Jr., my fifth child, and I was pregnant with my sixth child, at thirty-six years old. Their father was still struggling in his addiction. Our relationship had gotten progressively worse due to his drinking and baggage, which caused his unresolved thinking and behavior issues. Of course, being locked up thirteen years, he had mental thinking errors as well as insecurities and needed to control everything since he had been told every move he could or could not make for the past thirteen years. He needed help and would not get it. But I did love him, so what was my problem? We had talked about getting married, but we both had uncertainty. I found I was pregnant about the same time he was accused of raping a woman. That woman, he had been with, showing her an apartment that his mother had for rent. What happened was, the woman had called his mother that night after the accused rape, instead of the police, with a threat, and his mother told her, if she truly had been raped, to call the police. The police came to my house, looking for him. He was evading arrest, staying away from our home and out of sight. We spent as much time as we could together with all the kids, until he was arrested.

Shawn, Shannon, and Stephen went to school during weekdays, so we met up with him Friday through Sunday. He was crazy in love with the children and now his own baby boy, DJ, and all the children loved him as a dad. It made sense because they never had a daddy around that they remembered. This went on two to three months, until he was caught, had a trial, and was sentenced. I was three months pregnant with his second child. What had happened was, he picked up a woman that was going to rent an apartment from his mother. They had sex in that apartment, and she accused him of rape. Subsequently, he was charged, convicted, and sentenced to sixty-nine years for nine counts of rape, with a release date of 2028. This story is not about him. I share this with you because it is such a significant part of my story of transformation. At first, being pregnant with our second son during this emotionally overwhelming time. We had planned to wed prior, but now I was ashamed, embarrassed, hurt, and angry, so I thought, *No way. I will have an abortion. I can't love him and have his baby, because he doesn't love me.* At that time, I was the most selfish, self-centered child of God in the church. I was sick physically and mentally as well as spiritually for months as I thought about aborting.

One day, I had a conversation with a friend and sister in Christ who had had an abortion many years prior, and she told me it had been haunting her life ever since like a heavy dark cloud. So I decided to trust the Creator and have the baby. After I let go of the idea to abort and surrendered to the plan of God, the one who gives and takes life, I had such a peace, joy, and sense of wellbeing, not another day of anguish. Our beautiful son Daylin was born June 1994, ten pounds, eight ounces, twenty-four inches. He was my only C-section birth. We had weekly visits with their father at Chino State Prison; that was where Darwin first saw his second baby boy, behind glass. It was important to me that he and his children have a relationship, so I made every effort possible, being so familiar with daddy issues. Darwin asked me if I would marry him when he first got arrested. He said he was sure that the jury would find him innocent and he would prove to me he did not do it. That did not happen, and he asked me again after being found guilty and sentenced to sixty-nine years. I told him, "No way. I could not."

One day in the car, after I had had many conversations about this with the Lord, Pastor John McArthur was on the radio, a station I listened to for years daily, preaching on love. Agape, unconditional love, God's love, true love. I heard him say, when God gave His only Son, Jesus, that was love, and when Jesus gave His life, He stretched out His arms and died on the cross—that was love. True love hurts. It gives and is unconditional and sacrificial (no matter what). It seems I wanted to love and be loved my whole life but I didn't really know love. That was not my kind of love, and God wanted me to have and know the difference between His true love and what I called love. God said to me, "If your love is not like My true love, then it is not love. Call it something else, anything else, but stop calling it love." If you believe you love, then it needs to look like this: 1 Corinthians 13. God used this relationship with Darwin Sr. to teach me true, unconditional, sacrificial love for another and change the condition of my heart from selfish to selfless. To learn this, I had to practice disciplining my heart to put my love for my Lord Jesus toward Darwin. Loving on Darwin unconditionally, sacrificially, doing everything a good, faithful prison wife does, with no strings attached. I didn't think it was in me, but I was willing to change and do this new thing. I believed I was pleasing the Lord. Dying to self was hard, uncomfortable, unfamiliar, but it drew me closer to God and separated me from the self-centered, it's-got-to-be-all-about-me person that I was. Sanctified me for Himself, freed me. It was an awesome time of growth. "Greater is He that is in me than he that is in the world" (1 John 4:4).

Our second son, Daylin, was born the summer of 1994. I was preparing to marry Darwin while he was serving his time in prison. I sent my mom to the Hall of Records to get a copy of my divorce papers from Little Daddy. Records of divorce from my first marriage to Little Daddy, now sixteen years later. What I found was shocking. Mom told me I was told I was still married to him. After sixteen years, he and I remained legally married. Because after the judge granted the divorce, there was an error found on the document, so the divorce was not final or filed. That did not stop me. I married Darwin anyway, because that was what I wanted, and that is what I do, please myself. A really bad habit of judging according to my flesh. As an unforeseen human mistake, there was an error on one of the final forms that had to be corrected that caused our divorce not being filed into records. I married Darwin knowing I was still married to Little Daddy. The following year, January, Darwin and I were married at Calipatria State Prison in the presence of our families and friends. That allowed us to get monthly conjugal/family visits. That year, June, Daylin turned two years old. We went for a family visit, and his dad had gone way out, for being in prison, with birthday decorations, cookies, and cake to celebrate. Life was good and simple. Those were the good old days. Six years clean, and the one thing I was sure of was God made the difference. There was no lack. I was pleased with the way I was raising my children, secure, stable, peaceful, and content. The joyful, blessed life for my children, the best I had to give, with God's faithful gift of grace.

Thorn: Shannon was somewhat different; she saw life through less-childlike eyes. She had some residual effects of my addiction. She was made the second in charge from the very early age of seven of her three other brothers. She even cared for her older brother, Shawn. He was slow developing. While I was growing up and learning to step into my place as a nurturing parent, caregiver, teacher, and provider. At this point of the process, I didn't know what I was doing. But God's grace and mercy were there, and I was now hopeful concerning my children's future. Shannon was cheated out of her childhood because of my lack. I taught my children as I was taught. You can't give what you don't have; all you can give is what you have. The older children were to care for the younger siblings, every able hand on deck. What I do take from this is the way I raised my children was not all bad; it has shown to be not a complete liability but also an asset in producing leadership abilities—problem-solving, strong, responsible, and independent individuals with stability and respect for themselves as well as others. If I had known better, I would have done better. My compliant child developed some good character and control issues with it that made a conflict between us when it was time for her to let go, as I was better and ready to take my position as mother over the home and all my children.

Rose: Now seeing more clearly, I had no more doubt about how twisted and ungodly my thinking and behavior patterns were. My ability to manipulate and deceive myself and others to get what I wanted, ignoring the cost. "What is highly esteemed among men is an abomination in the sight of God" (Luke 16:15). "What profit is it to a man if he gains the whole world and loses his soul? Or what will a man give in exchange for his soul?" (Matt. 16:26). I, just a babe in Christ, was becoming more aware of a change in me because the people that had known me longest were watching curiously and would say, "You are not the same. What's up with you?" I didn't know how to communicate to them then what I have come to understand. The truth of God's Word was at work in me. I was in the process of transformation. Transformed by the renewing of my mind (Rom. 12:2). New values and beliefs were changing the way I lived and the things I did and no longer did. It was a slow change, little by little. Remember, I told you I was the Lord's most retarded daughter. However, when the Word of God got ahold of me and I got ahold of it, that began my change. First Peter 2:9 told me, yes, the Lord sees me as "special." His own special people, a royal priesthood, and God protects those whom He has adopted into His holy family.

> "And be not conformed to this world:
> but be you transformed by the renewing
> of your mind, that you may prove what
> is that good, and acceptable, and perfect,
> will of God" (Rom. 12:2).

Matthew 6:33 was given to overcome being retarded. Seek the kingdom of God and His righteousness. That means to desire more than anything God's righteous rule in life.

I had to receive my new position, identification from darkness—sin to light—righteousness, and line up my walk, conduct to represent my position in Christ (Eph. 5:8–11).

God is a rewarder of those that seek Him, receive His gifts of life, righteousness, and honor. This means a more abundant life (Prov. 21:12).

My ungodly thinking and behavior pattern of pleasing self no matter the cost, deception, was still in me. I moved to Yucaipa. Compared to every other place I'd known, there was a point on the freeway on the ride there that Yucaipa seemed like paradise on earth. I thought it was paradise compared to Los Angeles, after coming to Montclair in 1988, and then to Chino in 1992, where someone tried to kill me and my four children with a firebomb and gun. We lived in a really nice apartment in Chino after the fire, managed by the San Bernardino County Housing Authority. After Daylin was born, we qualified for a larger house, had outgrown three bedrooms. One clear, sunshiny day in May 1995, I was shown a house in Upper Yucaipa, a place I had never heard of, twenty-eight miles west before Palm Springs. The city sat upon a hill four thousand feet, with lots of hills, trees, and open spaces. I thought it to be a piece of paradise on earth. The house was wonderfully perfect, big front yard and back-yard, fruit trees, shade trees, fenced-in yard, no carpet—that was the best thing—two bathrooms, four bedrooms. The neighbors were good, kind people. Yucaipa was just perfect. Yet I was holding on to some old ways, idols. My hustle was insurance fraud, setting up accidents, a skill Little Daddy taught me. We moved there in August. Shawn celebrated his eleventh birthday that month on August 21. Friends and family came to our new house.

Rose: Life was good and simple. As they say, "Them was the good old days." I had seven years clean, and one thing I was sure of was God made the difference. Because the number of children I had increased by two while we lived in Chino, we were moved to this bigger house in Yucaipa. There I was placed on a program called From Welfare to Self-Sufficient, as my income increased. Eventually, my income consisted of Bobby's Social Security for the children, employment of two jobs, all the increase over the initial rent I paid when I moved in, which was $140. The rent increased to $800. All this was put in an account for me with interest, allowing me to go from renter to owner. God's goodness, mercy, and grace were all over me. When I first moved to Yucaipa, my income came in after my bills were due, and I acquired several late fees and bank overdraft fees monthly. They were costing me more than I could afford. I went into the bank one day, and the teller I had become most familiar with told me she was putting a $1,000 line of credit on my account. She must have had the authority to do it; I didn't know her position. I do believe she worked for the Lord, on my behalf. What she did for me made such a difference in my and my children's lives, being able to have full advantage of the income that the Lord had provided, not giving away needed hundreds monthly on fees. Now the bills would come in and were paid through the credit line. I was able to get out of that monthly hole. I will forever be grateful for her mercy and kindness and the Lord's favor in my life. I was overwhelmed with gladness and joy to be raising my children in such a good place. They were not so happy about the move, leaving friends, school, and all that was familiar to them. Stephen was bothered more than the rest. He had just finished hell week tryout for Pop Warner football and had made the team playing with twelve-year-olds, and he was only eight years old, due to his extremely large body. He had gained the respect of his neighborhood friends.

More Blossoms

Increasing the Fruit

Rose: When we first made Yucaipa our home, one thing that stood out was, there seemed to be very few black people. I was somewhat on guard after the fire experience. We attended a Church of Christ first for a short time. Because Bobby was a member, we had attended a Church of Christ also in Montclair and in Chino. What I felt was most important about where my children went to church was that the Trinity and the Bible were taught. At this Church of Christ, I received the Word, and the Trinity was taught. However, there were no others there like us, single mothers, on welfare, recovering from brokenness and addiction, although the people were welcoming. There were no ministries for us to fit in, although the people were friendly. We went to church on Sundays, but there was nothing else. We didn't attend there long. As we attended this Church of Christ, the Word was preached and people were nice, but no one identified with us. I felt like something must be wrong with us; we couldn't identify with any of them. I tried to befriend them, but I could not openly share with them. When I decided to leave, the pastor said he was so sorry because he needed those like myself to help comfort those that had my same testimony as the Lord sent them. That was what the church was for.

I do not believe in coincidence, and that same time, while I was taking a computer class offered at the Redlands Community Housing Authority, I made a friend. She and her mother worked there. She was white but had mixed-race children. During a conversation, sharing our testimonies, they invited me to their church. My children and I went the following Sunday. Immediately upon arrival, I was reminded of a party. The parking lot was crowded. There were people greeting and directing you, with big smiles on their faces. They helped me with my children; seeing Shawn having difficulty walking, they got us seats. As I watched in awe, the people standing, praising, clapping, and dancing, a young man, maybe aged eleven years old, rapped scriptures. The chorus of the song, which I will never forget, was, "Open the book yell, you've got to open the book." As the services went on, I could see and hear the spirit of love. God was there, the Bible was preached, and the Trinity was honored. We had found a church that my children enjoyed going to. Set Free Yucaipa Ministries, with a faith-filled man of grace, the shepherd Pastor Willie Dalgity, and his sweet wife, Marsha. I called the pastor of the Church of Christ where we had been attending and met with him to tell him we were changing churches. He responded with disappointment and asked if he could change my mind. I thought, if it were just me, maybe, but my children wanted to go to Set Free. There we didn't feel out of place, and there was so much offered. We started attending church four days a week. We were there Sunday service, Wednesday Bible study, Monday youth ministry, Friday community outreach, and Thursday Sisters in Service. Set Free Ministry Yucaipa, where it was all about Jesus. Sinners welcomed; no prefect people allowed. Where we are trained to serve Jesus 24-7. Set Free is an outreach ministry where men, women, and children come to live for free while they got to know Jesus and be free indeed (John 8:36). There were people like me and my children. Yes, there were also very few black people, but there were single mothers; people recovering, broken, living on welfare or poverty level; men with prison records; and those with a criminal history. At Set Free, this was the last stop for many of us; we had tried to be a part of society and been rejected or failed many times.

Rose: I loved my new life; caring for my children and serving God through people was what I did. My life was so different. I now saw some truth, the purpose and significance of my life. I was amazed with the value and confidence I felt. The Lord God Almighty was close and present in my life, nurturing me with His amazing love, exceedingly abundantly, more than I could have imagined. I heard a message one Sunday in church, Matthew 25:14, about stewardship. The master who went away and left his servants, three of them, in care over his business. One, he left five talents, the other two talents, the third one talent, to manage while he was away. When he returned, the servants were brought in to be accountable to the master for what he left them to manage. The one with five doubled his to ten, the one with three doubled his to six, while the one with one had buried his and had not managed it well. He made poor excuses and blamed others, yet the master said, "To those who have been good stewards of what they were given would be given much. To him that had not, all would be taken from him." What I received from that Word, which I believe was meant for me, was that God has given us all something to steward over. He is coming back, and we will be accountable for all He gave us. Everything I have, He gave me. Most importantly, my children and their souls. Also, I had all my daily needs met in abundance. Therefore, I went to Pastor Willie and told him if he knew of a woman who needed a place or food; I had more than enough for my kids and me and enough to share. From that point, there was always someone living in my house.

The first was a godsent, SG, with the voice of an angel and heart to match. She was also in recovery, a mother of two. Her son, a young adult, and a daughter that lived with her father visited on the weekends. She worked a job and was very clean, with an encouraging spirit and outgoing personality and was fun to be around. We became as close as sisters. She had been in the church for years. She was married to an abusive man with an addiction. We nicknamed him Pastor Crackhead because he knew the Bible and would teach it powerfully when not actively involved with drugs. He was incarcerated when she moved in and joined us when he was released.

I was employed at that time as an in-home support service provider for elderly and disabled people, assisting them so that they could maintain independently living on their own. Then I started my own small business, Chambers Complete Property Services, employing some of the disciples of Set Free. I started that business first cleaning my sister Renee's house once a month. She worked for a hospital, in administration. When the ladies she worked with mentioned they needed a house cleaner, she gave them my phone number. I received many of my clients like that. And I cleaned the office of the Redlands Housing Authority. I was also managing rental properties for my mother in-law. I served as treasurer of Set Free Servants for Christ and also served at the San Bernardino County Housing Authority on the resident advisory board. I needed to be available at all times for Shawn because of his disability and was blessed to be working around my kids' school schedule. I never knew when I would be called to school about Shawn, and his doctor's appointments were frequent.

Rose: Remember, I have told you, don't forget that I am still retarded and in the process of change, by definition a slow, incremental, step-by-step process. Life was good. I was better but still a long way to go regarding the deep things of God. I married Darwin Sr. at Calipatria State Prison on January 1995. Daylin celebrated his second birthday on June 1996 with his daddy and our family. We had a weekend overnight stay, three days, two nights. Darwin Sr. made all the decorations by hand. It was special. We would visit prison almost every weekend, it seemed. I was a good and faithful wife.

I did everything a God-fearing, loving wife does to encourage her husband to be the best man he can be and care for the family unit while providing financially for everything. Providing for the telephone bills so that we stayed connected and husband felt like he was having an input in the outside affairs. Also the prison packages, so he felt loved. And the visits, maintenance of the car. Make sure to pack the right kind of clothes and colors for the children and self. Wake up to drive in the middle of the night, gas for the trip, hotel fee, and money to buy food while on the visit and during the weekend for the family. Since we were there, we must stay for Saturday and Sunday visit and be forgiving when he called, talking crazy, because he had a dream I was with another man. This was the life I chose, week after week, year after year. You can't imagine what it is like explaining why I married him and why I stayed married to him, especially after the crime he was found guilty of. But I did and am proud of it, because I believed God was at work, and He was pleased with me.

> "Greater love has no one than this, that he lay down his life for another" (John 15:13).

157

The Lord's Best

I have told you these things, so that in me
you may have peace. In this world you
will have trouble. But take heart! I have
overcome the world.

—John 16:33

Consider it pure joy, my brothers, whenever you face trials of many kinds.

—James 1:2

Blessed and enviably happy are those
who mourn, for they shell be comforted.

—Matthew 5:4

Who, when he had found one pearl of
great price, went and sold all that he had
and bought it.

—Matthew 13:46

God's peace is the treasure of treasures, the pearl of great
price. It is an exquisitely costly gift, both for the Giver and
the receiver. The Lord God purchased this peace for His chil-

dren with His blood. We receive this gift by trusting Him in the midst of life's storms. With the world's peace—everything going our way—we don't seek God's unfathomable peace. We must learn to thank the Lord when things do not go our way, because spiritual blessings come wrapped in trials. Adverse circumstances are normal in a fallen world; expect them. Rejoice in the face of hardship, for God has overcome the world.

Shawn celebrated his birthday on August 1996. He turned twelve, with all his favorites—new clothes, toys, friends, family, and lots of food. He loved being the center of attention, dancing and singing; if there was a stage, he would perform. In September, he had a heel cord extension surgery to improve his balance when he walked.

In November 1996, one Sunday at church, when the pastor gave the benediction, while all heads were bowed and eyes closed, Shawn accepted Jesus Christ as his Savior.

Rose: I was delighted and surprised as Assistant Pastor Tree came to where we were sitting to get him, rolled Shawn in his wheelchair to the front of the congregation, and questioned him about his love for and belief in Jesus as the Son of God. Shawn, with his angel-like, beautiful big bright smile that lit up the room, answered all the questions. There is no coincidence in the life of a child of Christ! December 19, 1996, Shawn went to sleep, took his last breath, urinated on me as I held him in my arms, and died. Absent from the body, present with the Lord (2 Cor. 5:6–8).

Completely devastated, in shock. What was going through my mind was, *This can't be happening. Not now. Why? What did I do? I've been good, serving, tithing, faithful, no men or drugs. Why, Lord, why?* I still had compromise in my life, and some old idols. I had an insurance scheme going, another old behavior. I call it *compromise*, trying to get more money, which was an idol in my life. I had scheduled to meet with and get my money from an attorney at a local McDonald's. Shawn was out of his cast and recovering well but had a cold. I gave him Tylenol after dinner that night. We'd had Whoppers and fries from Burger King. Shawn consumed two. I was anxious to go and get the money waiting for me. I put the kids to bed so I could run out. I hate thinking about the last interaction I had with my son. He was in the way of me getting to my money. I was mean and impatient with him, yelling and cursing when I left. I asked SG to check in on Shawn while I was out, saying that I wouldn't be long. Stephen went with me. When I got home approximately one hour later, I asked SG if she had checked on Shawn. She said she had and he was sleeping. I went in to give him a kiss good night, and he was very still. I tried to wake him up; he didn't respond, so I picked him up in my arms face-to-face, and he exhaled a deep breath and peed on me. I did CPR while calling out for SG to call 911. They came, tried to resuscitate him, and put him in the ambulance. SG's husband drove. We followed the ambulance, and all I could do was cry. *Why? Why? What did I do? I'm doing my best ever now, God. Why?* Then my thought shifted. *I don't want to do this. I can't do this. I'll jump out of the moving car on the freeway and kill myself.*

Philippians 1:20–23 describes the strain of my dilemma, "betwixt two desires." Thank God for SG and MG; without them, I would have been all alone in my new surroundings. I see now that the Lord, who was not taken by surprise by any of this, sent them to me for a time such as this. This is how He has provided for my needs, through people He sent me to care for. SG was there to stay with my kids, and MG was there to drive me and sit with me at the hospital. My mama and sister Renee did come with their broken hearts, shock, and denial. They didn't want to accept it, but I knew Shawn was gone even with all the machines on him. I sat there hoping for change, but none came. It was December 19, DJ's birthday, and Christmas was approaching. I thought about my other four children I have left at home that needed me, and just before morning, the doctor came in and told me there was still no change, no brain activity. I gave my permission to pull the plugs and watched as the machines and his heartbeat and breathing stopped. I told Shawn how much I loved him, that I would miss him and never forget him. I told him how sorry I was, how much I wish I could change this. I asked him to forgive me, told him about the beautiful life he was going to have with Jesus in heaven. I told him to tell his daddy, Bobby, and his brother Waymond I loved them and I was so sorry. I kissed and hugged him one last time and left.

I went home to love on my babies and help them process the death of their brother. Again, I was confronted with the irreversible pain and regret of the consequences of my sin, my choices. This would be the last time I'd talk to someone I loved, someone precious to me, one I never wanted to live without. I was mean, self-centered, unloving, impatient, uncaring, and I couldn't take it back. First, Bobby, now Shawn.

Thorn: This put the light on my mouth, which shows my hard heart once again, and the consequence is pain. I seem to be the kind of person, although retarded, that learns from consequences. When something hurts me enough or cost me enough, that tells me there is a problem. This has been one thing I've learned about myself since surrendering to Christ. It is explained in one of my favorite quotes: "People don't change until the pain of staying the same is greater than the pain of change." I hurt too much to stay like

I was. I must change the way I talk to the people in my life whom God has placed for my good, knowing I will stand accountable for building them up or tearing them down. He loves me, and I must love others. They are valuable souls to God, and I must agree with His ways. James 1:19 says, "Be slow to speak, quick to listen, slow to get angry." This would also be the last insurance scheme I would take part in. Because of the Christmas and New Year holidays, we had Shawn's funeral the seventh of January. If it is true as I believe that a homegoing service is a direct reflection of that person's life, then it is safe to say Shawn lived the life he was purposed to live to the fullest. In his short twelve years of life, he touched, influenced, and affected so very many people. It was a sad but glorifying service, with remarks of his angelic, larger-than-life presence.

I have been blessed with loving, precious people in my life. I am so grateful for Janice and Langston; she is such an angel. They came up to Yucaipa from Los Angeles to make sure DJ had a birthday party. He was turning four years old. Christmas was hard, but so was our life every day living without Shawn. There was an abundance of everything—family and friends, food and drink, gifts and money, laughter and tears. But our hearts and minds were discombobulated. Someone so important to our lives was not in his place. We just existed, going through the motions of living.

According to the official death certificate, Shawn's death was due to "possible complications of cerebral palsy." I believe Shawn's CP was caused by one of two things, my fault, my smoking crack while carrying him through my entire pregnancy. Even though none of my other two out of three children, conceived and carried under more severe crack consumption, have it. Another possibility is, my addiction caused my high-risk pregnancy, a condition called toxemia, which caused the doctor to induce my labor, several different days from Augustus 10- to 21, for several hours, causing stress on my unborn baby boy that was already under stress, producing the lack of oxygen to his brain until he delivered. Either way, the guilt and shame was on me. I am so grateful for the Lord's forgiveness of sin, mercy, and/or I could not bear all the horrible, ungodly sins I am responsible for.

Thorns: These circumstances did show us that our priorities were and had been wrong. Christ Jesus's birth and His death and resurrection were the only light, hope, and joy for us. All the other stuff—Christmas music, trees, lights, ornaments, candy, foods, drinks, dress, and gifts—meant nothing. In preparing for the funeral, trying to be there for the other kids to help them process, it was a blessing to have SG and MG there; it was a lot to do. But God, the joy of the Lord, is my strength (Neh. 8:10). God, He was with me. He was so close I felt like He had me cradled in His arms, in a way I had only dreamed. I needed Him so much.

Rose: The Word tells us, and I have experienced it personally, where the Spirit of the Lord is, there also is strength, peace, joy, chastity, self-control, gentleness, charity, patience, kindness, wisdom, freedom, and hope, fruit of the Spirit. That which was my worst, weakest time became my best, strongest, most victorious time. I felt as if God, my Father, was carrying me, comforting me in His arms, cradling me in the way I had desired to experience since I was a young child. He never left my side or my mind. He put a constant song in my heart of praise, of His loving-kindness, and of His promise of faithfulness to me and my children.

Rose: So when the witnesses, like my sister-in-law Laneicha, came to help me as I mourned to go through this grief and loss, it compared to none. What she saw, she could not believe was possible. After being with me for some days before and after the funeral, she stopped me and asked me how I was able to do all that she had witnessed. How did I lose my son, care for my other children and family members, arrange and pay for his funeral, speak encouragement to everyone at the funeral, have so much peace and joy in the midst of it all? I gave her the only answer I had, Jesus, my Lord, and the truth of His Word. She responded then, "I want to know that God, the God you serve, because the God I know doesn't have that kind of power." I shared with her my testimony, Galatians 2:19–20.

A short time later, after she had returned to her home, she called me to come get her and take her and her children to the Set Free Ranch. Her man, the father of her two youngest sons, was not ready to let go, concerned with what he would do about preserving his worldly possessions. She let go and surrendered her life to Christ. God made something good out of that mess. Shawn died but brought life for her and her family, and there is no way to know how many others until that day when we reach heaven. Her man later joined his family at the Set Free Ranch after being counseled to put his things in storage and trust God.

Rose: What I am telling you is, there is a power in perception, a different, new way of thinking, believing, and being that can be found in the mind of Christ. *Thorns on the Rose* is a depiction of the power of receiving a new prospection. With Shawn's passing away, I thought I was going to die if I lost a child, that it would kill me, and yet I did not die. But God, I gained a supernatural strength to live on through the love of Christ Jesus. One night, days after Shawn's passing, I was still in that quiet place in my heart, continuously asking the question, "Why, Lord, why this? Why now?" See, I believed I deserved this kind of pain before, but not now. My loving heavenly Father, who knows me so well, gave me

SHERON CHAMBERS JEFFERSON

an answer to my question. I know He didn't have to, but He loves me like that. He knows me and all my ways; He deals with me accordingly. I was in my bedroom, in my bed, asleep yet aware. I saw Shawn in the bed with me, as he had been so many times before. It was overwhelmingly real. Everything was so familiar. I felt his presence. I smelled his smell that was like no others, yet I was aware that Shawn was gone and this could not be real. When I looked closer, I saw he had one of those haircuts with words shaved out in his hair. The words were "Glorify the Lord."

Rose: That was my answer from the Holy Spirit. He went on to tell me that I have one primary purpose in life, and that is to glorify the Lord, with all that I am, in everything I do, and with all that He has given me. He went on to speak to me about my using Shawn's disability as an excuse when I didn't want to serve God. I had told the Lord I wanted to serve Him to use me, but I used Shawn when it wasn't comfortable or convenient for me. Also, that money I was tithing, thinking He was pleased with me because I was giving large amounts, was not what He wanted. He wanted my best, and that was what He died for, all of me. He said, "Come all the way in without excuses and compromise. He said I had been standing outside the gate, with my lame and bruised offering to the Lord." Come all the way in so that I will reap the fullness of His benefits. The initial and ongoing spiritual work of deliverance of God in our lives is the shaping encounter for how we relate to God. More specifically, as we'll see, it formed the basis of the Spirit-formed, Spirit-filled, and Spirit-used life. Of little consequence to God, however, is your perception of these experiences with Him and how the Holy Spirit seeks to use a delivered and filled person in the lives of others. As we'll see that God goes to great lengths to deliver His people from any Egypt. He desires that they translate their deliverances into meaningful service for Him. Thank You, Father God, for showing me how intent You are on shaping my truth in regards to being less concerned for my children than my money. I needed to be delivered from a spiritual stronghold for money, greed, and the spirit of poverty.

God has a Holy purpose for all suffering and heartache. To make us better people. Poet Robert Hamilton wrote, "I walked a mile with Pleasure; she chattered all the way; but left me none the wiser for all she had to say. I walked a mile with Sorrow, and ne'er a word said she; but oh! The things I learnt from her when sorrow walked with me." Here is another truth: "In the darkest night, we seek the stars. In our sorrow, we are driven to God. Certain life lessons can be taught through sorrow. Sorrow is a gate we must pass through in order to experience God's happiness. As gold is purified in the furnace, so is the faithful heart purified by sorrow" (Robert Browning Hamilton).

Rose: This junction of my spiritual walk, this amazing and significant experience with the Lord Jesus, with these circumstances and situations that allowed me to know the love of God, changed me. His ways are higher and better, changed my very existence, from the inside out, and exposed the God in me. I was learning to live with new values and beliefs, guided and directed by the Holy Spirit. My disposition toward people and circumstances was changed, from an excitement for the journey to an ever-growing relationship with God.

> "Whoever has the Son has life; whoever does not have the Son of God does not have life" (1 John 5:12).

The Unseen Buds
Preparation

While under the teaching of Pastor Willie, it was made clear that I was called, chosen, predetermined to be a disciple. Discipleship is born of obedience. Disciples are people who hold on to Jesus's words as their law of life. People who acknowledge Jesus as master of their life. One who has been given a task, saved, and set free. Jesus is glorified through His disciples; as God sent Jesus, Jesus sends His disciples to lead the world back to God again to give them a new awareness of God. Jesus offers His disciples two things: joy and a warning, making them different from the world, by everything He says to them. And when we endure, we will experience Christ's love at its best. So my desire to be independent and self-sufficient, following my own will, had to go. God has His plan, His destiny for every person; we can accept or decline God's plan for our lives. "They were Yours, You gave them to Me and they have obeyed Your Word" (John 17:6). As disciples, we become aware of the voice of God in Jesus's Word and observe God's hand in Jesus's actions. Quoting Henry Ward Beecher, the strength and happiness of a man consists in finding the way in which God is going and go that way too.

Rose: In the fall of 1998, I was permitted to take part in starting a new church in Atlanta, Georgia, with a group of disciples from Set Free Yucaipa. We went by bus to Atlanta, Georgia. The plan was to do exactly the same thing we do weekly all over the county of San Bernardino: find a place where people were, fire up a barbecue pit, put some hot dogs and hamburgers on the grill, go out among the people, and talk to them about Jesus and the good news, invite them to eat while someone shared the message, and offer them all who would a new life with Christ and a ride back to Set Free Yucaipa Discipleship Ranch. Pastor asked all of us that were heads of a ministry to each be speakers to deliver the Word to the people. I had been given the privilege and honor as president of Sisters in Service. On the bus, I was praying and asking the Lord what He wanted me to tell the people. For days, I studied and prepared to speak from Hebrews 2:3, "How shall we escape if we neglect such a great gift as salvation?"

The day after we arrived, the pastor came to me to tell me my family had called him and asked him to tell me my sister Vaughn had passed. I called home to find that she accidentally overdosed on pain meds given her due to a knee surgery. This was another painful consequence that I could not take back, that forced me to change. She and I were complete opposites, but our sister relationship was deep. There was nothing she could need that she couldn't get from me, and vice versa. We made it a point to get together weekly and enjoy each other's company. We would go out to show off our amazing height and beauty. She lived with me several times. And after I started having children, she was there to help and would take them with her for a day. But you see, she and I, my sister just fifteen months apart, had not spoken in about a year, for such a stupid reason.

Thorn: I thought I had learned my lesson with Bobby and Shawn, using my words to tear someone I love down and leaving the hurt unresolved. My sister had no children, and

170

I had five. During a family gathering, as my children and I approached the door, she said, "Here come Sheron and her babe babes." We got into an argument, said mean things, and stopped speaking. We once had been so close. I made more of an issue out of that than was necessary. I believe if we had been speaking, she would have called me and not have died alone. No more will I allow a conflict to separate me from a loved one. I will forgive and seek forgiveness. There are no coincidences. The message I had prepared from Hebrew on the great gift of salvation, and the danger of neglecting it, was meant for those at Vaughn's homegoing celebration.

Rose: The good news was, we knew where she was because she had escaped, received salvation. The question was now to her loved ones in attendance: "What about you? How will you escape and see her again?"

Rose: I enrolled in college the following summer of 1999. As a member of the Board of Counsel of the Redlands–San Bernardino County Housing Authority, I was asked to share my story of recovery at a meeting. There was a Substance Abuse Program Director that attended the meeting. After the meeting, he took me aside and offered me a job, paying $12 an hour, good pay at that time. But he said I would need to take some drug/alcohol classes first and get certified. School was the last thing I ever wanted to do. At that time, I was receiving a welfare check and Shawn's Social Security check while working my own business cleaning private and commercial property, and also managing rental property.

Thorn: The name of my business was Chambers Complete Property Services. I made very good money and was able to be home with my children and work around there school schedule. But it was hard on me physically. I told my sister-in-law about the opportunity, and she immediately thought it was a great idea and enrolled. She had gained a great passion for recovery. She enrolled a semester before me and would tell me every day how much she loved the class, while trying to change my mind about going back to school. So the following semester, I enrolled, motivated by my sister-in-law, to prove that I could not do it. Living in the past of who I was, dumb, stupid Sheron. I found I was not the same, at forty-one years old, working, single parent of five children under the age of thirteen, with one remaining brain cell, in early recovery. I made the dean's list every semester of the five I attended. Because the information was so interesting to me and sometimes it sounded like the class was about my life experiences. It was like I had found my passion. I was not the same old person; this was the Lord teaching me to walk out the plan He had for my life in my new nature. "Therefore if any man be in Christ, he is a new creature: old things are passed away; behold, all things are become new" (2 Cor. 5:7). "But they put new wine in new wineskins, and they both are preserved" (Matt. 9:17). "Jesus called in a loud voice, 'Lazarus, come out!' The dead man came out, his hands and feet wrapped with strips of linen, and cloth around his face. Jesus said to them, 'Take off the grave clothes and let him go'" (John 11:43).

I Am Who and What God Says

Thorn: After two years of classes, in 2001, I was seeking an internship and instead secured a job as an in-custody substance abuse counselor at Chino State Prison, for Center Point Inc. This was the first real job I'd worked since 1981, Ford Motor Company. I had worked as an IHSS worker, with as many as three clients at a time, making pretty good money to subsidize my income. During that time, the Lord was at work, transforming my heart, teaching me to love with the love of God and drawing me nearer to Himself. I was promoted at my weekly women's Bible study, Sisters in Service, from treasurer to president. I invested more and became stronger in my recovery. And I started my own business, Chambers Complete Property Services, with employees from Set Free Ministries, which brought in a significant income, but it was very physical. Counseling behind a desk sounded good to me.

Rose: I loved the work. I was a good counselor. I made a difference in the lives of the clients and for the company and staff. I believe counseling is one of my God-given gifts. God used me in the prison system to serve and build His kingdom, to be light and love among the dark. By His Spirit, bring a new perspective, hope, and healing. Because of my long experience with men wasting their lives behind bars and the effects they had on the loved ones they had left on society.

My working in prison daily, going behind the wall through the bars that closed so loud, was an experience that is hard to verbalize. Until you have experienced it, you cannot imagine the heaviness, darkness, sounds, smells, movements, and details of the happenings there. Which is what Darwin would try to communicate to me during a visit when I asked about his daily life in there. The first year of our marriage, 1995, we had monthly conjugal visits along with weekend visits, if the prison was not on lockdown. The following year, the law changed and sex offenders no longer received conjugal visits. I continued being faithful to my marriage. The inmates were amazed to know that I was totally committed to him in spite of knowing the overwhelming circumstances. Darwin did not approve of my working in prison; he was angry and jealous because of his knowledge of the mindset and exposure to many men. He was not alone— the majority of my family disapproved. Everyone felt like I was in an unsafe environment, especially my father number 2, Jefferson. Myself, I had a sense of security and serenity, based on the confidence that it was the Lord that had purposed for me to be at that job, and anywhere the Lord sends me, He will protect me. I saw the Lord use me as an influence in many lives in there. I was known to be a woman of faith. Even though there is a law and a policy in prison not to use religion, I was singled out as the staff on our team. My boss brought difficult inmates to me for counsel. He knew I used the principles of the Word of God, and that made a difference, a positive effect. I got good at speaking the Bible, God's Word, without saying scripture and verse, believing His Word would not return void (Isa. 55:11).

My clients were very responsive and made significant changes in their conduct, behaviors, and attitudes, and ultimately their lives, which positively had an effect on the lives of their family members of society as a whole. In the in-custody SAP, which stands for Substance Abuse Program, the inmates were put in groups of twenty and selected group names to identify the individual groups. After learning of the process of how diamonds are mined and developed, my clients chose to name their group Diamonds in the Rough. There were clients and incidents that stand out in my mind, and I believe I did as the Lord would have me in producing lasting fruit. "So that whatever you ask the Father in My name, He will give you" (John 15:16).

So I was working and loving the job, feeling good about life, with my newfound identity in Christ, in my zone, living my purpose, and amazed at how far the Lord had brought me. After my sister-in-law graduated with her certificate of completion for drug and alcohol counseling, which I never received, she was seeking employment and asked me to talk to my boss about a position. I did, and she also came to work for Center Point Inc.

It was at this juncture of my journey that I found my true self, my identity in Christ. I am who Christ Jesus says I am. I found my competence, which produced confidence, and walked in my blessing to be empowered by the Lord to be in that position, to serve in my gift, promoted by God, not man. I found true sufficiency and confidence when I put my total dependency on Jesus. The Lord was changing me. "Therefore, if anyone is in Christ, I was a new creature; old things are passed away; behold, all things have become new" (2 Cor. 5:17).

I was living faithful and pure, honoring marriage, learning to love unconditionally with true love, God's love, a servant for Christ, joyful and content. There was still my very real issue of incomplete divorce papers from Little Daddy. I was not legally divorced from Little Daddy, so that meant I couldn't be legally married to Darwin, and I was living a lie before the Lord. I was so confused by deception.

"God is not the author of confusion" (1 Cor. 14:33).

Confusion and mistakes come when we forget the importance of God's Word as our unwavering guide.

I deceived myself into believing I was living according to the Word. I had forgotten the lie I had created and was living. I was never a free woman to marry Darwin. Remembering that I was not married according to the law of the land made filing for divorce easy; after all, I was still married to Little Daddy. I made up my mind the day, about ten years into the marriage, after my DJ was on the internet and typed in his name and up popped his dad's picture, on his dad's web-page from prison. An enticing picture of his dad standing in our bathroom, with only a bath towel around his waist. That happened to be my favorite picture, advertising for a pen pal. His bio had no mention of wife or children. When I asked him about it, he had no remorse while stating, "A man's got to do what a man's got to do." That was the end for me. I was once again hurt, rejected, and betrayed. I told him he would be sorry, and never would he look into my eyes again. I quit communicating with him and let go of the relationship completely. The Word is true all the time. Matthew 13:9–16 speaks of having ears but not hearing or understanding, and having eyes and not seeing. Those who want to hear and see the truth do, but there are those that don't want to receive the truth by hearing or seeing; they will not. That was me. I learned something very important about myself. I was such a deceiver, liar, manipulator, pretender, and whatever else name you want to use, but I didn't only deceive others but also myself to get what I wanted. That was what a broken, self-centered person I was. God still had a lot of changing/ work to do on me (Phil. 1:6).

I must tell you, I fell so fast for Darwin; I only saw what I wanted to see and heard what I wanted to hear. It was years after we married, had two children, lived together on the streets, and had many years of prison weekend visits. I was having a conversation and was asked to describe Darwin. While I was doing so, Shannon said, "Don't forget his missing front tooth." In surprise, I said, "What missing tooth? Does he really?" The person I was having the conversation with asked, "How could you not see that?" I've come to understand that was not what I was looking at or where I was focused. This was only the beginning of my evident need of character, most importantly integrity.

Thorn: I met another inmate in 2004! While working in Chino State Prison as a counselor, though not his counselor. One of my clients brought him to my office and recommended he talk to me. I remember when I looked at him standing at my office door, he was full of darkness. I could see it in his eyes. He said he needed to talk to somebody. He talked, I listened, and I presented different scenarios he might consider. He kept coming back. Eventually, I introduced him to the Bible, pointed him to a scripture. He came to my office before or after his own counseling group almost daily. I could see he had a lot of hurt, fear, shame, guilt. He seemed hopeless and suicidal. I talked to his counselor and the program director regarding the sessions I'd had with him, and they both thought it was helpful that I continue. As he continued to seek the Lord, studying the Bible and putting it to application, the light seemed to come on, and there was change. It was obvious to everyone, his peers and the staff. In 2005, while preparing for his release, he told me he had fallen in love with me, through poems, and whatever I wanted him to do, he would do. All he wanted was to be part of my world. I knew he had feelings, from all the attention he showed me in letters, pomes, and cards. I was supposed to report him to the prison authorities but never did. I encouraged him to go to an aftercare residential drug program, where he could focus and strengthen his recovery and relationship with the Lord. He agreed but asked if we could spend his first day out together. I agreed, as wrong as I was. I had compromised my integrity, ignored all the rules. I was trained for this and knew when he started showing feelings for me, I should have stopped counseling him and reported it. I must be truthful: I was flattered, and I was curious to see how the sex would be. I had been celibate thirteen years. We did spend his first day out together. It didn't bother me that he was twenty-two years my junior. I was forty-eight, and he was twenty-six. However, he hid that for as long as he could. That he was an ex-inmate and I was staff. That I represented God as a woman of faith and living righteous, and that this was wrong on so many levels. Nor did I consider that this was my second relationship with someone who had repeated incarcerations and many strongholds and generational sin. I didn't ever give a thought to the possible harm this could have on him. None of that mattered, only pleasing the lust of my flesh.

In 2005, I stopped working at Chino State Prison as a substance abuse counselor. I went out on a medical leave. First, I was under a lot of stress while trying to care for my father, who lived in Los Angeles after having a stroke, and caring for my own family, who lived in Yucaipa, San Bernardino County, ninety-mile difference. Added to the stress was my involvement with this man, who was in Chino, an inmate, and against the rules and my ethics. My sister-in-law also worked there and lived just down the street. At that time, she and I were not getting along well. I felt she owed me because I was instrumental in her recovery; we had gone to school together to be counselors. Also, I was the one who brought her résumé to my boss, which got her the job. Then she was promoted above me. Then the state mandated that all counselors be certified. I asked her to use her certification to falsify records for me. And she told me no. I didn't take no well. I stopped speaking for a long period. What I did not realize was that my recovery was at risk because my integrity was jeopardized, and I wanted her to compromise hers. I was so wrong. I do believe that our integrity is the boundary that protects us from going back to who we were, and no one is worth that. She did admit that she owed me and asked for a dollar amount she would pay me. Of course, I did not want her payment, and then I would miss God's reward. Later, I discovered that with my years of counseling at Set Free Campus, I had more than enough hours to qualify for the certification. God had already prepared me to be and to do what He had called me to do. I learned some very valuable lessons from this experience. While on leave and meeting with a therapist weekly, being the know-it-all that I was, with a few psychology courses under my belt, I learned that I suffered from irrational thinking, expecting others to be like me, to treat me like I treated them. I was wrong to place my expectations on others. Also, I had not cried since the loss of my first son, Waymond, twenty-six years earlier. I stopped crying to stop feeling. I thought it was a sign of weakness, and nobody cared anyway; it was my own fault. And crying doesn't change anything. Again, I was wrong. It is human to cry and feel the emotions that accompany tears. "Jesus wept" (John 11:35).

Genesis 1:26–28 and Solomon 2:23 tell us we are created in the image of God, and tears, He created and gave purpose to mankind, emotions and tears. And not to have tears and emotions is to say God is wrong and would be unnatural and inhuman. I also learned that my oldest, deepest sin of selfishness, self-centeredness was not gone, and God's work on me was still happening, and I must do my part to have a support group to be accountable to. Lean not on your own understanding. Examine myself daily and upon awareness of old habits, unhealthy thoughts, thinking patterns, or behaviors. Stop, confess, and repent; turn from pleasing my flesh and toward pleasing the Spirit of God (1 John 1:9; Acts 3:19; Prov. 3:5).

That same year, my father number 2, ST, got sick and later passed away. He had made me executor over his Trust, with three houses, furniture, car, and more money and responsibility than I had ever imagined. It was three years prior my father number 2, ST, after the passing of his wife, asked me to come over his house after work one day. There with his attorney present, he told me how sorry he was for choosing his marriage over a relationship with me all these years, and now he wanted to right that wrong. His Estate Attorney and he explained that my father wanted to make me executor of his Trust, that worth more money than most people see in their entire life (six figures), and explained what that entailed to do so I would need to change my last name to Jefferson by signing the forms he had. I felt a lot of emotions stemming from the history of the relationship. I was angry that he would ask me to take his name now that I was over forty years, when I told them I wouldn't change my name. Sheron Chambers is who I am, and have always been!

The attorney said I didn't have to change my name. I could add Jefferson, so I agreed. I really didn't believe I would be the one to inherit everything he and his wife had accumulated. Especially the way she felt about me. And I had such a severe issue with inadequacy, feelings of insecurity, rejection, never feeling good enough to be the winner. However, I did and really enjoyed it. One of the most difficult things I encountered was paying my tithes. I was a weekly thither of 10 percent, but when I calculated 10 percent of that check, the truth of my faith was revealed. It took me a moment while trying to rationalize and justify with the Lord. I kept ending up at the same place. He'd say, "You still don't trust Me?" I would think how that must disappoint Him and how He deserves so much more from me. So I obeyed His Spirit to trust Him. I felt real good about it. I learned a few things about having money, like it takes more than two million and skills to manage it in order not to run out. It will bring the worst out in people; it's not all good or all bad. It takes the sting out of being poor.

My son Stephen was preparing to leave for college. We made it a road trip, he and I, one last opportunity to strengthen our relationship as he took on his next level of maturity, entering adulthood. With Stephen having been man of the house most of his life, I told him on our way to Sacramento State University about TH. Stephen, representing the man of the house, said he would meet him on the basketball court to determine his acceptance of him.

The first weekday of TH's release from prison, he went to report to the parole office, which happened to be in Inglewood, the same city my mother lived in. I was at work and received a call from my mom. She said, "I have a surprise visitor, and he brought me a beautiful bouquet of flowers. Guess who." And she passed him the phone. When I heard his voice, I was shocked. "TH, how did you find my mother's house?" I asked.

He answered, laughing, "I have my ways."

Spooky, but I was impressed.

His following day pass away from the program, he went to see his mother in Venice, and then to the Santa Monica Pier, to have my name tattooed across his chest. Again, I was very impressed. He did put a lot of work into showing me how serious he was about me.

When Stephen came home on a school break, he and TH met on the court for a one-on-one game of basketball. TH, twenty-six years old, six feet tall, 190 pounds, street baller from Venice, California. Stephen, nineteen years old, seven feet tall, 275 pounds, Sacramento State College, scholarship, starting center. TH beat Stephen three out of three games, and at the end of the game, TH asked Stephen, "Who's your daddy?" We all laughed, but from that moment on, Stephen called TH "Pops." They had a great relationship. It was also in 2005 that I stopped working at Chino State Prison as a substance abuse counselor. I went out on a medical family hardship and did not return. It was at that time I also decided to "pull my grace card" and filed for divorce from Darwin. Contemplating marriage to TH, never giving the fact that I was not divorced from Little Daddy a thought. We were already living together, like I was doing something differently, like I had never done this before. There is not enough time, paper, or words for me to explain how stupid I have been when it comes to men. Here it is again, that deception, self-gratification, self-centeredness, and lust of my flesh that had caused me pain too many times for me to repeat this sin. Regarding being divorced from Little Daddy, I was led to believe that the system would have put the divorce through due to the extensive time that had passed, now twenty-six years since the court ruled. God's Word is true, no matter how long it takes me to believe it. "He who sows to the flesh will of the flesh reap corruption. He who sows to the Spirit will of the Spirit reap everlasting life" (Gal. 6:8). This Word, *the* Spirit gave me loud and clear, and I responded, "I hear You, Lord, but I want him."

The Lord was continually clearing out old trash from my life. I surrendered and laid my life at the altar; however, time after time, I didn't stay there. My flesh was not dead and was still reigning (Joshua 24:15).

During a casual conversation with my princess, Shannon, that same year, my only daughter, now twenty years old, I can't remember exactly what we were talking about. I made the statement, "You know I have your back. Haven't I always been there for you?" She dropped her head and became silent. I repeated, "Haven't I always been there for you, Shannon?" She then looked up at me and said, "No, Mama." I was completely unable to breathe, in shock. When I was finally able to speak, I asked, "When was I not there for you?" and she answered, "When I was a little girl, I told you WC touched me between my legs, and you didn't put him out for touching me." After what seemed like hours of processing my shame, guilt, and remorse, I admitted to her I was wrong and was so sorry for not making her know that she was the most important to me. I was wrong for not making her feel safe and secure. I was wrong for not caring or being more aware of her feelings all those years. I asked her to forgive me. She said yes. I am so grateful.

TH and I married in 2006. He proposed, full on, with a ring he painted three houses to buy. That night was my birthday. We had planned to go to dinner with my daughter and her baby's father. Early that morning, he called her and asked if she had time to take him to get my birthday gift. She told him she would be by in a while, but he was so anxious he rode my son's bike down the hill three miles to the jeweler's for the ring, then to the florist for roses and rose petals, then to the market for cake and balloons. Can you see this picture? Pedaling up the hill, you have to love him. When I walked in the door after work, he and my two younger sons (twelve and thirteen years old) met me, singing happy birthday, with cake and candles. When I blew out the candles on the cake, I noticed rose petals leading down the hall to my bedroom. He took my hand and asked me, "Do you trust me? If so, close your eyes and follow me." He led me down the hall through the rose petals into my bedroom, then told me to open my eyes.

I opened my eyes to a room filled with burning candles and rose petals. There was a huge red rose in the middle of the bed. As I began to focus in on the activities around me, he began to speak. "There is something I want to say to you, and as God has told me how to love you in the poems I have written to you for the past three years, this, too, is God, not me. I have never done this before, but God told me this one thing that He will tell me how to love you." As he began to pray, he asked God to bless His purpose. He prayed for every part of my body, from my head to my feet, and that God would anoint and use them for His Kingdom. When he finished, he looked me in the eyes and asked me if I would allow him to love me like Noah loved God. He then asked me if I could name the most beautiful flower there is and picked up the big red rose from the bed. We spoke the answer at the same time, "This rose!" Then he began to open the petals, which revealed an engagement ring in the middle of the rose. He asked if I would marry him. I answered yes! My two youngest boys, DJ and Daylin, were so happy for him to be in their lives. They said, "We finally get to have a dad."

There were many events that bonded us together. We shared my father's passing, and he was the one my daughter went to first to tell me she was pregnant with her second child.

We were having a good time, enjoying each other, together all the time in the beginning. We shared a lot of intimate details about ourselves; our conversations went on for hours. We complemented each other. Where I am responsible, consistent, and structured, very detailed and serious about making sure all needs were met, the business was handled, taking care of everyone in the households needs, the financial manager, he was a hard worker, generous, fun, and spontaneous. We decided to meet with the pastor for marriage counseling. On our first visit, the pastor said, "You are already living and sleeping together. Sheron, I love you. You know the Word. What can I tell you? If you guys were not sleeping and living together, then I would counsel you." We left his office. I had served for years over the women's ministry at Set Free Yucaipa and now living in sin. So I removed myself and confessed my sin before the church. TH and I did agree to stop sleeping together until we got married, and he moved out of the bedroom. But that didn't last long. Once we were married at Set Free Yucaipa, with the whole church, our families, friends from Chino I worked with, the celebration was on with God's permission. He made the rule that we would wear no clothes when in our bedroom. He loved me, overweight and all; it showed in his face and all his actions. It was not all good and not all bad. I am sharing this because it didn't last. He was back to his addiction and then in prison a year into the marriage. His going back around his triggers, old people, places, and things, led to using drugs. He was in and out of jail. I'd put him out and take him back. We went back and forth until he went to prison for three years in 2009.

All my strongholds from my father abandoning me and other childhood wounds, the lies and maladaptive behaviors they produced, that overrode my spirit man once again. I gave in to the flesh. My way of loving, not God's way, not an unconditional covenant. So his addictions started to get the control of him, anger, being nice, and then anger again, until I let go, gave up. He was under the influence of darkness, living totally ungodly, in and out of jail every other month, until the inevitable happened. It was 2008. He was locked up again while he had been arrested three or more times and released and also sentenced to complete drug rehab. Which he did not do, even though he had many privileges there, because I got him into the Set Free Program.

He had just completed three years in prison because of his strongholds, addictions, and hang-ups. That was where we'd met. I thought, *This can't be. I cannot do this. It's wrong on all levels.*

Mama, My Mountaintop Experience

His being locked up was a relief for me, because at this very same time, the summer of 2008, my mother had a severe stroke. My brother called and told me Mama was in the hospital. I rushed to get there. I had to wait to see her after the doctors examined her. The report of the doctors was that she had a stroke with a brain bleed, affecting her right side. When I got to her, she was talking, alert and aware. She told me to help her up and get her out of there. She looked fine, but her right leg was weak. She was insistent and demanding that she could walk if I helped her up. This was her second stroke. Of course, I had to tell her no; I felt bad, and she was angry. From there they put her in a room and bed, administered meds that put her in a coma to release the pressure on her brain. My family sat together in that waiting room, praying, hoping the situation would change soon. It got bad while we waited. Between us, real quick, arguments and contention broke out. I am the sixth of seven children, and I was the only drug-addicted, single-parent, welfare-recipient, low-income renter. And the one most like Mom. My mom and I had a very special, close relationship, even more so since we both had been born again and transformed. It was in the hallway of the waiting area that my young teenage nephew gave me an understanding that made me aware of the change in the dynamics of our family. He pulled me away from the group and said, "Auntie, you can't act like them. You are the spiritual representative of the family." I believe the Spirit of God sent me that message through the least-likely person. "Out of the mouth of babes and sucklings you have gained strength" (Ps. 8:2). I received that message, turned from my flesh, and put on Jesus. Sometimes I have to remind myself with the song that says, "I need just a little more Jesus to help me along the way." Repeating until I am in the mind of Christ.

Mom was in a coma for what seemed like a month, as the three of us that prayed for her recovery, accompanied by family members, friends, and the church. This was her second stroke, and she was eighty years old and had already been blessed to be the USC's oldest recorded survivor of lupus. When she got saved and changed her way of living and became a servant for Christ, God made her a miracle. She was given six months to live by her doctor in 1970, but she lived fifty-one more years. When she came out of the coma, she was moved to a rehabilitation hospital, where she was until we found that she was being mistreated through a couple of incidents.

You see, Mom's mind stayed sharp, but the staff there didn't know that she could talk. The staff were giving her morning baths with cold water. Once, I went to visit and she asked me if she could have the gold cross I was wearing around my neck, so I put it on her. It was an expensive piece of jewelry TH bought me. A few days later, I came to visit, and it was gone. I asked her what happened to it. She said the same mother-and-daughter team that bathed her with cold water in the morning took it. My family filed a report that the director tried to minimize, but we requested to meet with him. When we did, he said it probably mistakenly came off when they were changing her. I spoke at that time and told him what Mom had said, and he stood still in his tracks and responded, "Thank you. I know what you are saying is true. There is a rule here against family working together, yet there is a mother and daughter that work the early shift. Tell me the price of your necklace and I will have a check for you tomorrow."

The final straw was when we found my mom with bed sores. The director asked that we give them some time to see to it that the sore was gone, and they would not charge for the last sixty days. We agreed but still reported them to the overseeing authority. We started making plans to take Mom from their home. When we as a family talked about whom she would live with, everyone was willing, but it would take more sacrifice for some than others. Due to jobs and the house being two story and getting her upstairs or not having enough room. So I asked her, "Mama, we want to take you out of here. You have six children and places to go. Where do you want to go? Whom do you want to live with?" She looked up at me with her big beautiful hazel-green eyes, pointed her finger in my face, and said, "I wanna go with you." I said, "Then that's where you will live!" My mom lived five months with me. It was a lot to do. All my family helped to make sure she was as cared for and comfortable, and lots of her friends visited. I arranged to take her on outings in a transporting vehicle, because she was completely unable to move herself. She loved the mall at Christmastime. We took her out to see the lights and decorations. While we were there, I told her she could have anything she wanted. She wanted to go to Macy's. There she picked out a cross with diamond necklace and diamond earrings. She had always liked expensive things.

She was so happy. I had her room festively decorated, and Christmas music was playing. The door of her room looked like a beautiful, giant gift wrapped with a big red bow, and on the bow was written, "The gift in this house." Knowing she was not going to be here always, she and I had always talked about "going home" and looking forward to heaven and all the Lord's promises. Up until she left here, we shared the Word and our hearts with each other. She told me she wasn't ready to leave her children. I told her God was not going to take her until He was sure she was ready. She told me she hated being a burden on me. I told her how she had blessed me, allowing me to show her how much she meant to me. She allowed me to lay down my life for her. Caring for her in ways she was unable to do for herself. She liked Häagen-Dazs ice cream a lot, but doctors told her it was not good for her heart condition. Mom said she was going to die from something and would not give up ice cream. My older sister, Renee, doing what she thought was best for Mom, refused to buy it for her, but I let her have whatever she asked for. She wanted her favorite candy bar, Snickers. I would chew it up for her and feed it to her like a baby. And watermelon, I put it in the food processor. She loved cold watermelon juice. Showing her love like she had done for me and taught me to love. Her care was my priority, and my privilege.

> "Greater love has no man than this, that
> a man lay down his life for his friends"
> (John 15:13).

I will never forget or regret that time. It was an amazing journey, as unreal and serious, life-changing; all the decisions and sleepless nights, I knew God had us. His Presence was there and so real. I felt peace and empowered by the Spirit. At the same time, I took a call from TH, as he was still fighting his case. I told him I was done, that unless he was willing to admit his guilt, take the time being offered, and agree to substance abuse programs offered in prison and truly surrender his life to the Lord, I was filling for divorce. I had also been contemplating having weight loss surgery, the lap band, paying cash in Mexico. A date came available December 27, and I went accompanied by my angel, Janice. My daughter, adopted daughter, and my sister stayed to care for Mom until I returned on the thirtieth.

"But the fruit of the Spirit is love, joy, peace, kindness, forbearance, kindness, goodness, faithfulness, gentleness, and self-control. Against such things there is no law. Those who belong to Christ Jesus have crucified the flesh with its passions and desires. Since we live by the Spirit, let us keep in step with the Spirit. Let us not become conceited, provoking, and envying each other" (Gal. 5:22–26).

It was like we were separated from the world on a mountaintop. It was similar to Shawn's passing, how the Lord had me cradled in His arms. My mom pass away January 3, 2009. Early morning at seven o'clock, the night nurse was leaving and the day nurse came in, gave her medication, and cleaned her up. She was on hospice by this time, heavily medicated, so she would not wake up but passed in her sleep peacefully at home. My sister Renee and niece Tracy had stayed over so that they would be there when it happened. I went into her room. Her head was lifted up from the pillow, and her eyes were wide open, big as saucers, like a deer looking into headlights. I don't know what she was looking at, but she seemed amazed! I yelled to the nurse, "Why is she awake? She's supposed to be medicated and asleep!" The nurse, also puzzled, said, "She should be asleep." Mom exhaled, lay back on her pillow, and closed her eyes. Everybody in the house came and stood around her bed. She opened her eyes again wide, while inhaling a deep breath for what seemed like several minutes. Then I told her, "It's okay. Go to Jesus. We will see you soon." She exhaled and closed her eyes. I had made her a promise that I would not let her be buried without her dentures, so I was asking the nurse, "Can I put her teeth in now?"

"Not yet," she answered.

Mom opened her eyes and inhaled, like she was beholding His Glory, while we said our goodbyes. That was the last time we would see her big beautiful green eyes, and then I put her dentures in.

That day, after her body was removed from the house, our sister Janice prepared a birthday party for my brother Sam, because Mama passed away on his birthday. Days following, the Spirit said to me, "You have been to the top of the mountain, where it is pure and clear. You were separated from the world and its contaminants, and now it's time to come down. I promise you that the blessing I have for you will be a bigger blessing than what you received on the mountaintop." I have no idea what the blessing is that God has for me; however, I trust and look forward with great joy and expectation for whatever the God who gives good and perfect gifts blesses me with (James 1:17).

Living to Be His Joy

From the time I had come to believe that it was true, I could live free of mind-altering substances, that it was a lie that I would live my entire life and die an addict. I wanted to tell everyone that lived and thought like me that there is a way out. I wanted to open my own faith-based recovery program. Now some twenty years later, 2009. So I did, now that I had money, time, now that Mom was gone and all my children but Daylin had left the house. He was in junior high school; the two older boys were away in school.

Stephen's away in college, on his third scholarship at Oklahoma Panhandle State University. Stephen was my baby conceived and delivered when my addiction was at its worst. I told his father we shouldn't have this baby, that it was going to come out a big white rock. It is hard to admit this out loud, but I believe it will help someone who is like I was. Someone tired of being bound, blind, self-centered, selfish, the lowest of the low, to cry out to the Lord Jesus and trust Him with your life. The report of man said that due to the circumstances Stephen was born in, Stephen would be small in size, with malnutrition, unhealthy, subject to strokes and heart attacks, if he delivered at all; the baby would have brain damage, mental illness, social handicap and be in and out of jails. However, the report of God said differently. My son was born ten pounds, twelve ounces, twenty-four inches long, in perfect health. He has never been arrested. He has graduated college with a bachelor's degree. He is seven feet tall and has played college and pro basketball, traveling all over the world. He has a nonprofit organization coaching, using basketball to teach life skills. He is also an elementary schoolteacher at a Christian school. He is a man of integrity, caring, loyal, wise, compassionate, with great sense of humor and lots of personality. He is a hardworking husband, father of four (same mother), big brother, friend, neighbor, and he loves the Lord Jesus. Whose report will you believe? (Luke 10:17–19).

The Lord had blessed DJ with a full scholarship to a $50,000 a year prep school in Connecticut. At fifteen years old, my second beautiful, athletic, six-foot, ten-inch basketball-playing son was recruited to South Kent High, a faith-based school on the other side of the world. That was a hard decision to make as a mother. It came down to, Have I taught him everything he needs to know to leave home, and if I have, would I want him to miss an opportunity like this to keep him with me? My answers were, I have taught him all he needs to know, and if he were home with me, he would be practicing what he has been taught and he can do that there under the supervision of the coach. So the decision was his, to take this privilege and opportunity to do what he said he wanted. He and his brothers had been playing organized sports, baseball and basketball, since seven years old. During our talks, we used to say, "You can be the man with keys to the gym or the man who cleans the gym." I told him it was up to him and I supported whatever he chose. In my heart I wanted my son with me. However, I knew his character. He is able, strong-willed, adventurous, and fearless. It was a hard yes. We hugged and cried together. I bought everything he would need—prep schools wear, suits. I got our airplane tickets, and off we went. I needed to see how, where, and who would be accountable for my son's living. He did well, as I know he would, traveling all over the East Coast.

My baby boy Daylin, the child the enemy has been trying to destroy since conception, was fourteen years old at this time, in the ninth grade in Yucaipa, California, six feet, seven inches tall. Needless, all his peers were small in size comparably and white. When like every other day during lunchbreak, as usual, the smallest boy in the group picks at the biggest boy in the group, repeatedly hits Daylin with a ball and runs away. When Daylin finally catches him, to show him how small he is, Daylin picks him up in the air over his head. As he is putting him down, the small boy is squirming, and Daylin drops him and his arm breaks. Two fourteen-year-old boys horseplaying, and the police are called and criminal charges are filed and Daylin is expelled from the district with a restraining order to stay away from all school playgrounds. Now you must see what I was saying about the enemy trying to destroy his life. He was ordered to take anger management classes and had to teach himself that semester. I would pick up his books and assignments and test. So when the district called a meeting with the police and district psychologist to determine if he would be allowed to attend high school in the upcoming year, the Spirit spoke to my prayers. "Trust in the Lord with all your heart, and lean not to your own understanding" (Prov. 3:5–6).

Everyone was saying, "Don't worry about it. It's going to work out." You know what I truly did? I got an attorney, a very competent, sharp white female. She met with us, heard the story, and said, "That is pure racism," and said she would love to take the case. Her fee was fifteen thousand. This was no surprise to God. He had gone before us and prepared the way. At that, I probably surprised her when I pulled out my checkbook and wrote the check. This was a very stressful trial because they were hurting my child. They were slandering his character, lying about, trying to rob him of his future, and if they had had their way, they would have. With a criminal record for violence, expulsion, no college would have considered him. When the meeting took place from the time it started, the truth was revealed. The records on him since he started school told what kind of person he was. The district started with what they thought would protect them from liability. So they came at Daylin hard, saying they felt he was a threat to other children, so the police interjected that they refused to press charges for an accident that happened during the horseplay of two fourteen-year-old boys. Then the math professor for the district spoke, saying Daylin had a remarkable mind, while teaching himself his ninth grade. He not only had As all his test, but the test the professor had been using for nineteen years. Daylin is the first student to point out that the question is wrong; therefore, you cannot answer it correctly. It would be a great injustice to Daylin and society to follow through with this. Then my attorney spoke, reminding them that he had perfect attendance since the kindergarten, an A student, and had had no incident reports. He was a perfect student that you want to expel and ruin the life of for being black and for his age. If you don't return him to classes completely cleared of all accusation, I will file a discrimination lawsuit and have it on your desk Monday morning. More than a conqueror (Rom. 8:37, Isa. 41:10, Deut. 31:6, Matt. 28:20. The following year, a prep school in San Diego, California, gave Daylin a full scholarship. To God be the glory! I've been told by high school coaches that statistics show that 10 percent of high school seniors in California get one scholarship, but my three sons have had three and more.

They have turned down scholarships. I don't want to come across like a prideful brag, but there are ways to tell, evidence of God's blessings and favor in your life. Praise the Lord!

We started with two rooms and four empty beds. My sister Renee and I were like Moses and Aaron. She had the gift of administration, while I had the gift of counseling. There was also my best friend, JJ, who had the extensive experience in and with recovery treatment programs. We got busy. I took classes, got the necessary documentation prepared, filed for a business license, and started His Joy Recovery Treatment. What we offered was different from the majority of programs because our focus was recovery, not the treatment. In the beginning of treatment, a recovery program focuses on the disease, causes of abuse and addiction, traumas and events, and the learned behavior and thinking patterns, cause, and effects of such as these. Then one learns tools and life skills to manage said thinking and behavior patterns when triggered to give the individual options.

But our program focused on clients in their third and fourth phase living out daily the practice of prioritizing their choices, Jesus, others, and then yourself, to live a life of trans-formation/recovery, using everything they'd learned in phase 1 and 2, powered by the Holy Spirit to train. As I reflect, looking back over my life, seeing Jesus's beauty, compared to the beauty of the rose, which has been developed in me. His examples are my goals, like caring for others, nurturing, encouraging, listening, being fun, positive, and passionate about building the Kingdom. My main focus is developing a closer personal relationship with the Father God through the Lord Jesus. I pray continually as a result of the privi-lege this relationship allows. His is my days' priority; my day starts with setting first time for the morning prayer, medita-tion, and reading Scripture alone in His Presence. I choose to live each day with a positive attitude and a clean heart. That is not automatic but comes from years of practice and commitment. The more knowledge I gain of Him, the more my expectations of man are lowered, and the more my peace increases. Practicing acceptance of myself and others based on His Word and the value and love He has for me. I also practice doing a daily inventory each evening, with prayer and Scripture, to avoid drawing from my own limited perspective and understanding, to receive from God's limitless wisdom. I keep a journal recording the positive things I did and what good things I was blessed with, giving myself some credit for what was accomplished by His Grace.

I review my mistakes and promptly admit where I was wrong and ask for forgiveness and guidance in the matter and repent.

My relationships are healthier. I am able to admit responsibility for my part of the problem, as I have been made clear where I sinned. I have a part. I am changing me, my part. I don't plan to be married again, but I don't know the plan God has for my life. I have not divorced TH. There is another man for me, the lover of my soul, Jesus. Looking at the journey of my life, I have sought relationships to ease the pain of growth, creating another addiction, using the relationship like a high, putting distractions between me and my priorities. My immaturity, an unhealthy mindset, prevented me from knowing what a healthy relationship is or how to have one. All I have known is how to possess, invade, demand, attack, and conquer. I love the honeymoon phase but have been incapable of sustaining the most important factors of a relationship. I have been blessed by the Grace and Mercy of God that my emotions connected to "relationship" have not caused me to relapse in my sobriety or turn back from my transformation. I have changed my whole life and these past twenty-seven years. It was all or nothing, not lukewarm. I planned to come all the way into this new life and not look back or bring any of the old life into the new. Making the choice daily of what I allow in my eyes, ears, mind, and heart. By challenging old values and beliefs, I have changed my behaviors:

From	To
Dishonesty	Honesty
Doubt	Hope
Procrastination	Action
Fear	Courage
Taking the easy way out	Integrity
Complacency	Willingness
Cockiness	Humility
Expecting too much from others	Love for others
Lacking discipline	Self-discipline
Lacking responsibilities	Perseverance
Compromising values	Spiritual awareness
Lacking gratitude	Service
Omnipotence	

Most importantly, the attitude is gratitude. Eventually, I have learned not to support and nurture my unhealthy thoughts and to monitor what is going on within. I never dreamed I could be as disciplined and live a normal life and still be me and really turned on and alive! I have gained an inner peace I never thought possible. I, to date, have realized that through all I have suffered, I have been most richly blessed. And God is still at work in me. It's not over; I'm not completed. The journey continues. In spite of the thorns, God is creating a unique, authentic, beautiful rose with the most wonderful fragrance, vibrant color, so large and full of life, with one-of-a-kind, detailed markings. The rose?

My children are all young adults now, thirty and twenty-one. In January 2014, I invited them to a weekly CA (Cocaine Anonymous) meeting, where I was presented a cake and a chip representing twenty-six years of recovery. I would be the meeting's speaker, sharing my story, encouragement, and hope for those in the room. Shannon, twenty-eight years old then, my eldest and only daughter, with Daylin, twenty years old, my youngest son, and Shannon's children, my grands, Sanaiah (nine) and Shon (seven), came. Shannon and Daylin presented me my cake, and I shared what I was led to. My journey, where I was, and where I had come from when I surrendered to God, and the events that had the biggest effects on my recovery and transformation. I shared a lot. It was not the first time I had shared it, but it was that first time I shared it all at one time in front of my children. It felt freeing for me to be vulnerable, to be clean and free after so many years of working to overcome my past. Although the uncertainty was off, the response was real.

I finished my speaking, and the meeting attendees asked questions. We prayed out. As we were walking out, it was very quiet. Daylin spoke, saying how surprising that was; there was so much he never knew about my life before Him. Shannon tried to speak, but all that came out was loud, uncontrollable sobbing. She fell to her knees. People came to see if she needed help. She continued for twenty minutes before she could speak, then she said, "I never knew you are the reason my dad died. All these years, why didn't you tell me?" I told her I was ashamed and felt guilty. For the past twenty-six years, this has driven me into the arms of Jesus. I am who I am today because of this. I didn't just decide one day to be a Christian; I needed saving, a Savior, Jesus, to face myself in the mirror, to face my children, whose father I helped kill, to face life. I hated the person living in my skin. I am saved because I needed a Savior, and this was the life event that God used. I told her, "I was protecting you and myself. I did not want to add more hurt to your life by telling you that not only was your mama a selfish, low-down, retarded crackhead, but also add that you were conceived and birthed while I was active in my addiction, as well as your brothers, and maybe why Shawn had cerebral palsy and died maybe due to the effect of it. But to add to that, your mama encouraged your daddy to smoke crack and set that addiction off, and he was killed because he was trying to get more and chose not to stop. And I was protecting myself from the fear of how this would affect your love for me. You say I should have told you. If I had told you when you were younger, do you think you would have processed it better, if this is your response at twenty-eight years of age? I am sorry. Will you forgive me?"

She looked at me and said, "I have to go. I don't know how to deal with this. I love you, and I will talk to you later."

The following week, I called her just to say, "I love you." During that time, she talked about it with Stephen. His reply to her was, "Mom has, for twenty-six years, lived to make amends for her past. Let it go!"

Looking back over my life, I see, when I looked for God, He helped me. He comforted me and blessed my life with His Love, Grace, and Companionship, and the more consistent I became at calling on Him, the more intimate the relationship became. He was my help, comfort, and companion. As I recognized my need in Him with small matters and in large ones, my spiritual relationship was kept alive. His Love has comforted me like a child cradled in her father's arms through many tragedies: my Shawn's death, when my house was burned down, my baby's father cheating, convicted of rape, and going to prison. I married him and loved him ten years, and he cheated again. Then my sister Vaughn's, my father's, and my mother's deaths. These have been some of my most precious times of solitude, peace, comfort, assurance, and growth! Through these I have felt comforted to be a comforter through whom God comforts, comforts others. I have been told many times, by friends, loved ones, and those that know me and have a relationship with me, as well as complete strangers that I have contact with, that I have a presence and my hugs are something special, feels like a mother's hugs. Since I am a hugger, I have a presence that calms, soothes, and comforts a person. The best hugs. That makes me doubly blessed. I receive some of that comfort that flows through me. The ultimate riches of Salvation has been God's constant companionship. No matter the loss I have experienced, nothing can take this gift from me (Ps. 34:4–6; 2 Cor. 1:3–4).

Moving forward through the adventure I know as life, there is ongoing privilege and opportunities to learn and grow from. I have come to understand an awareness of the name of Jesus. God said in the book of John 14:13, and Philippians 2:9–11, and told the apostles to pray in the name of Jesus. It's more than just a phrase; all that God is and does is represented in the name of Jesus. Learning that has taught me that all suffering has meaning for the building of His Kingdom. All my pain and problems are and have been opportunities to build a true, recognizable trust for God. To be set apart as a vessel of honor for the Lord. Learning this fixes my attitude on gratefulness. Being thankful to the Lord for all my suffering is one of the highest forms of praise. With an attitude of gratitude by faith through grace, patiently suffering all things in the name of Jesus.

As my story has been told, you can see I have had my share of suffering, and when it strikes, I am reminded that God is Sovereign, and He can bring good out of everything. I have stopped trying to run or hide from problems, as was my old habit. That kept me repeating, stuck in negative consequences, low living, a vessel for dishonor, looking like a retard, unwilling to seek help and take the advice available to me. Until I surrendered to God what was His, started living to please Him instead of myself. Realizing I was not receiving the outcome I was seeking, recognizing my actions were not confirming what I said were my values, and I started accepting His ways were not my ways and were better and higher than mine and I needed a new mind and new perspective so I could change my condition and do and be better. I accepted adversity in the name of Jesus, offered it up, received it from God for His purposes. That changed my value of suffering, and it gained meaning and drew me closer to the Lord. God is a rewarder. I receive joy from the closeness of His Presence, and from the ashes of adversity through trust and thankfulness (John 1:2–4).

(Acts 20:7–24.) This journey has led me to realize that my receiving Jesus as Savior in 1988 (being born again) was not just to miss hell. My purpose was to please God. To lay down my life to fulfill His desires. To be His special possession on earth and to serve others and do whatever He tells me to do. It's all about Jesus; my top priority is to give myself to Him and to live in communion within His Presence. Spend time with Him that I can hear His voice and respond in obedience. In doing so, I am genuinely fulfilled, able to live the high life I've longed for. That the Lord is all I need when I need it. My deepest desires find fulfillment in Him alone. He has changed my self-centered attitude to becoming totally reliant and confident in Him. He has called me to take the high road, the road less traveled, in continual dependence on Him. The confidence I live is true confidence, which comes from believing the Bible is the Word of God, from God to me. It tells me I am complete in His Presence. Everything I am not, I lack; everything I need is in Him. And the mystery of the Kingdom of God is, "Greater is He that is in me." All I must do is hold on, not give up, and not turn back (John 15:5; John 14; Eph. 2:4–6). God is still working to change me, but today I don't resist His ways, growing spiritually. I have become flexible and teachable (Prov. 26:12), overcoming being arrogant, unteachable, unapproachable, prideful, wise in my own eyes. Through perseverance, today I believe God has raised us up to sit together in heavenly places in Christ Jesus, according to the Word of God. For too many, too much, and for too long, I have belittled what He did, by not living like Him, allowing Him to bring me alongside Him. That was God's purpose at Calvary, to make us what He was (exalted, one with the Father, having authority).

He put on a physical body, came to earth to gain authority over sin and sickness, demons, fear, poverty, and all the other curses that came when the law of death came into the earth, and He completed it on the cross. "It is finished" were the last words He spoke. We inherited all that He is when He gave up His name. He did it for you and me, so we could wear His name and hold and use His authority as a weapon or tool on earth in our life. He did it so that we could stand before God and be everything to Him that Jesus is. When we are born again, we are the righteousness of God in Christ!

Today, what I believe makes the difference in how I live. Being retarded is no longer any excuse for me. I ask God to reveal anything in me that is ungodly or unpleasing to Him.

He is the light of the Word that exposes all darkness. He answers my prayers, and I receive what He shows me. He has given me understanding regarding my laziness and fear and how it has hindered my spiritual walk and affected my life negatively many times in many ways. Being lazy has caused me to move slowly, the idleness and procrastination, to put off until another day or time. Quotes influence my learning. *The Purpose Driven Life* book taught me and helped me so much. One of the lessons on obedience used this quote: "Delayed obedience is really disobedience." Wholeheartedly obeying unlocks understanding. No partial picking and choosing the commands we'll obey while ignoring the ones we think are unreasonable, difficult, expensive, or unpopular. Partial obedience is disobedience (John 2:24).

Writing this book stands out in my mind when it comes to being disobedient for more than seven years. This also reflected on my being a poor steward of what the Lord has given me purpose, time, and opportunities to glorify Him (1 Cor. 4:2). Being faithful, a characteristic I value and possess today, full of faith that God has me here for a purpose. So each day I'm excited about starting the day with God, praying, reading His Word, connecting with Him, and journaling. This helps me prioritize, gives me a plan, and gives me direction to get me started. Through personal experience, I have found that fear can paralyze us and keep us from getting started. The fear of failure has convinced me in my past that I can't change. Why even try? It's no use. It's too late. I don't have anything of importance to share. Fear kept me in disobedience. I kept pushing aside good desires to return to school, start a business, get out of my rut of being comfortable in poverty, until God stirred me, encouraging me to step out on faith, take a risk, and trust Him. Believe His Word! He had already called, purpose-gifted, and prepared me to do what He wants me to do. I pray, dear Lord, that I don't want to miss opportunities and blessings because of disobedience due to laziness and fear ever again. Give me courage, hope, and a firm shove to move forward, pleasing You with every day of life You give me. I, at times, have been my own worst enemy. When I am walking and living according to my flesh, when I won't deny myself. I believe, as a child of God, I have an enemy, the devil, and the world. But my worst enemy, my closest enemy, is myself. For far too long, I have allowed my self-centered thoughts of what should and should not be, based on my emotions, that distract—fearful, paralyzed, mum, fearless, annoying to others, rambling, unintelligible conversation, incoherence, bad language, loss of train of thought, not understanding, difficulty paying attention, unbalanced, stumbling, difficulty walking straight, inability to stand, falling down, rudeness, aggression, being argumentative, offensive, having bad attitude, temperamental, violence, loudness, boisterousness, being confused, being disorderly, being overly friendly and motivated, losing inhibitions, and having inappropriate sexual advances. The emotions are disappointed, agonized, aggressive, enraged, grieving, guilty, lonely, lovestruck, pain, sad, suspicious, paranoid, perplexed, mischievous, indifferent, horrified, envious, disapproving, disbelieving, anxious, arrogant, confident, disgusted, distasteful, exhausted, frightened, jealous, miserable, negative, prudish, smug, turned on, undecided, withdrawn, regretful, obstinate, hurt, bitter, and angry.

Who told you that? I have shared circumstances and situations in this book that I, even as a born-again believer in Jesus Christ, the only begotten Son of God the Father, the Messiah, the second person of the Godhead, God the Son, feel it is necessary to be specific as to what I believe. I have found too often that when I ask someone, "Are you a believer?" and they respond, "Of course," when asked if they believe this about Jesus, they answer no. So they claim to be a believer, but a believer in a different god than the Bible teaches and that I believe in. That because I refused to obey God's Word and follow the example, Jesus, the Son of Man, set. By denying Himself, living to please the Father, bearing His cross. The factors that lead to my choice of disobedience are real, like everyone else's, reasons, or explanations, but not valid after I was born again, just excuses. When I cut away the factors and excuses, I am left with being self-absorbed. As a child, it was expected, acceptable, especially in a mind of the dysfunctional background, upbringing of strongholds and the wounds that were inflicted and the brokenness they caused. So when do we, I, stop being a child? (1 Cor. 13:11). When I was a child, I talked, thought, and acted as a child, but when matured, I became a woman. I put away childish ways. That seems to be an ongoing job, to put away my childishness. Making that change is when we grow up. Slowly, step by step, as I recognized familiar old thoughts, patterns, thinking, and the feelings or emotions that accompany them. It is here at this point that cognitively I must identify my choices before acting out on my emotions. I have improved with practice, choosing the best way, the high road, the mature way, serving God instead of flesh. I talk to myself, saying, "Burn the boat that you have used so many times to go back, back to a sin." The boat that I used for eight years while I decided life or death, a substance abuser/addict or child of God. The thought of the boat comes from when God took His people out of slavery across the Jordan River and some returned to their familiar, ungodly ways; they went back. I identified with them and thought I must burn the boat so I can't go back again.

Relapse with crack to crack addiction—people and things and places that have crack were the boat. The boat that kept taking me back to being sexually promiscuous, having no self-worth, needing to be wanted. Being a liar and thief for money and image. No integrity. The boat that kept taking me back to pretend to be someone other than myself, to feel good about myself. Need to be in control, everybody's provider, answer, with the fear of rejection, being critical and judgmental, hurt. Currently working still, but I want no more self-centeredness, which has caused me so much pain, with the death of my first-born son, Waymond; three marriages; a van for two times its worth; feelings of not being good enough; self-hatred.

There's one thing that has made the biggest impact in my change with understanding that my thinking, my thoughts, were the root of my problem. Where every idea was born. I began to examine, look at my thoughts. I saw that my mind had a way of thinking that judged every word in my vocabulary. My judgment of every word was connected to a perspective that was formed from an ungodly place, person, or thing. So I tested that theory. I took a word, any word, wrote out my thought of that word, and then looked that word up in the Bible to see what God says about that word, and it was never as I thought. The question arose in me, Who told you that, about that word? Then I had to look at who my teacher was, who or what taught them. Where did this understanding come from? All my information, my thoughts, were ungodly, false, temporary, or deceptive. So I started deleting my thoughts. Then resetting my thinking based on the Word of God and what the Scripture teaches regarding this. As I proceeded, I began to see the enemy (Luke 10:19) and how he has set me up as a young child, doing what he does, robbing, stealing, and destroying (John 10:10).

I was a captive of the enemy, my own worst enemy, fighting against the Spirit in me, therefore a defeated Christian. That is an oxymoron.

"Be sober, be vigilant, the enemy is seeking whom he may devour" (1 Pet. 5:8). Thinking that *sober* is confined to "under the influence of mind-altering substances" is narrow-minded thinking. I have experienced being under the influence of anger, lust, love, pride, greed, and hurt—i.e., other emotions that have altered my mind, stopped, and hindered me from being vigilant. I was so blinded, distracted, numbed, and unaware. When I came to myself, I had been devoured, beaten up from the feet up. Taking every thought and word into captivity to the obedience of Christ (2 Cor. 10:5). Replacing the ungodly thought with the godly thought taught me to stand up against the enemy, and he left me alone and went looking for whom he could devour (John 4:7). Resist the devil and he will flee from you (Eph. 6:11–16). Going to a battle without the whole armor of God—it's a spiritual battle. The battle belongs to the Lord. He has equipped you, making you complete, lacking nothing, that you may stand against, stand in the evil day, and having done all to stand. Stand therefore with your waist girded with truth, breastplate of righteousness, feet shod with the preparation of the gospel of peace, and above all, the shield of faith to quench all the fiery darts of the wicked one. The Lord fights the battle. He just wants to see my faith to trust in Him, to endure until the end and not give up, not let go, not turn back, but just to stand in faith in Him. He desires that I endure, and I desire to endure (John 1:4).

Micah 7:8 strengthens and comforts me today. "Do not rejoice over me, my enemy, when I fall, I will arise; when I sit in darkness, the Lord will be a light to me."

Perseverance must finish its work so that you may be mature and complete, not lacking anything. As a child, I was known to fall down a lot. Mama called me clumsy. Maybe that's why I fall down a lot still. The Scripture tells us there is power in the tongue; words speak life and death, blessings and curses. In my journey with Christ, I fall down, and I get back up again. It has been said that my life is like a rubber ball, up and down. I thank God for His Love, Grace, Mercy, and Faithfulness to keep getting me up. A righteous man falls seven times, but he gets back up again (Prov. 24:16).

Because of Jesus, I have overcome. I am an overcomer by the Blood of the Lamb.

Recognizing the trick of the devil, our enemy, that he set to destroy the life God has for me. Self-centeredness, self-pleasing, self-first, me, I, and myself—the problem. The solution comes in the form of a new mind, a new understanding, a new perspective (1 Cor. 7:31). Think differently, with the mind of Christ, and live different.

"The form of this world is passing away." All of it is temporary. My soul is eternal. Stop thinking so narrow-minded. Invest in what is eternal (John 1:9–11).

"This world and the lust of it is passing away, but he who does the will of God abides forever" (1 John 2:17).

My desires, values, changed as my thoughts changed, and therefore my activities have changed. "When the world perceives all is well 'peace and safety!' Then the destruction scripture has warned of comes upon them. And they shall not escape" (1 Thess. 5:3–4). But the church and the righteous, born-again, sanctified followers of Jesus the Christ, brethren, are not in darkness. Christ is the light. So this day should not be a surprise or should overtake you like a thief.

I thank God I am not one of them. I have a way of escape—Salvation!

"We see through covered lenses, one day, face to face." How we see life now is not real. The carnal world we live in is not as it will be. We, people, are not what we are meant to be, or what we are going to be (Heb. 11:5–6). The way to think and perceive and live is by faith. How? By the power of the Spirit of God, the Godhead, living according to the Word of God. That is where Truth is found. Where our understanding, knowledge, wisdom guides us, our lives, to the abundance of prosperity that He, Jesus, came to bring people back to, like Adam before his choice to disobey. We call it a successful life (Ps. 37:4).

The journey isn't so much about becoming anything; it's about unbecoming everything that isn't really you. Take off what the world has caused you to be, down to the original, authentic child God created you to be. So you can be who you were meant to be in the first place.

God's masterpiece—favored, well able, strengthened, generous, grateful, forgiving, confident, whole, beautiful, healed, successful, blessed, anointed, gifted, loved, victorious, unstoppable, determined, courageous (Col. 3:3). Your life is hidden with Christ in God. And this has put me on the path to desire Holiness. To be Holy, for God, my Lord, is Holy. "Follow Me," Jesus said. "Live like Me, please the Father, and bear much fruit" (John 15:1–8, 9:17). The vine and branches are an excellent picture of our relationship to God in life. We must be connected to be fed and nurtured, dead if apart from Him. Trim decay at times to make us lean and strong, abide/alive, remain connected, persevering; we produce healthy fruit in the form of love and faith. His Grace is sufficient; it has brought me from death to life, made a way when there seemed to be no way, transformed me and my way of living, brought me back to the daughter He created me to be. This poem by Russell Kelford sums it up:

You are who you are for a reason.
You're part of an intricate plan.
You're a precious and perfect, unique design,
Called God's special woman or man.
You look like you look for a reason.
Our God made no mistake.
He knit you together within the womb;
You're just what he wanted to make.
The parents you had were the ones He chose,
And no matter how you may feel,
They were custom designed, with God's plan in mind,
And they bear the Master's seal.
No, that trauma you faced was not easy.
And God wept that it hurt you so.
But it was allowed to shape your heart,
So that into His likeness you'd grow.
You are who you are for a reason.
You've been formed by the Master's rod.
You are who you are, beloved,
Because there is a God!

I look back on my life from where my eyes of my under-standing were enlightened, which means were opened by God, and I began to see how twisted my mind and heart were. How far I was from God, even as I was trying to be a better person. God had a better plan. God had a lot of work to do (1 John 4:18). I was controlled by fears as a result of unrealistic expectations, of being alone and unloved, of need-ing approval, of coming out of my comfort zones/change, of being judged, of failing, of competing. What I desired more than anything was to please God. In all the positions I had been given—mother, daughter, wife, sister, friend, employ-ee—I had to be a useful, effective, active participant of the church. I desired to be compassionate and loving, selfless, and obedient to the Word of God.

Little did I know that I had a lot of ungodliness controlling me, like guilt (Ps. 32:1) due to regrets of a lot of shameful things. So I was afraid to venture out, and I missed great opportunities, played it safe, avoiding risks, keeping me from becoming what God intended for me (Job 5:2). Anger and resentment for the hurt and pain that I didn't deserve, and it was not fair. Because I wouldn't forgive, I couldn't get over it, and so I became bitter (Matt. 6:24). The most obvious controlling force was my materialism, being greedy and hoarding—always acquiring more stuff was my goal. I believed that having more would make me happier, more important, more secure. But it's all not true. Just temporary satisfaction and fulfillment. My net worth did not heal my self-worth. My value is not determined by my valuables. God says the only thing of value is people. I was seeking security and self-sufficiency in money. Real security can only be found in that which can never be taken from you, your relationship with God (Matt. 6:24).

I was also driven by the need for approval, always feeling like the old odd man out, not good enough, not important, not smart, not pretty, just not enough—the opinions of others and what they thought consumed me.

These ungodly controlling forces led me to a dead end. Unused potential, unnecessary stress, and an unfulfilled life (Eph. 1:18–20).

Because of where I started, today I believe in transformation. Not being a little better, but completely changed, a new creation. And that is the driving force in my life today. I believe it's for me and anyone else that wants it. It's all about your willingness to depend and trust completely in the Lord for help. When I gave Him all my sins, as He showed them

SHERON CHAMBERS JEFFERSON

to me and how they kept me from the person and life He planned for me, one at a time, He strengthened me to trust Him, and I sought after Him more and more. "You will seek Me and find Me when you seek Me with all your heart" (Jer. 29:13; Ps. 105:4; Deut. 33:25).

Mankind was created by God for God's glory. At the core of man, in his foundation, there is a soul, an abyss, a hole, a space, an emptiness intended for God alone. If or when we don't fill it with only God, the space, the hole, emptiness, that abyss is filled by or with the enemies of God. But it will be filled by one or the other. Can you see? It becomes our choice based on our decision. That has been the problem for me, filling that space made by God, for God, with ungodliness. And everything humans do, every action, is a reaction; every choice and decision starts with a thought. Where the enemy works, our thoughts are influenced, influenced by perceptions, perceptions from experience—what we were taught, what we saw and felt, our senses and emotions, which are not truths. The carnal mind cannot receive the things of the Spirit, and the carnal mind is led by the things of this world. They change temporary feelings based from our senses, sight, hearing, touch, smell. They are not truth. The things of the Spirit are unseen to the carnal mind. They don't change; they're permanent and true. Because God was not Lord over my life, or my parents as a child, the enemy set me up with ungodly hurts, things that happened and wounded me, ungodly thoughts. Because I was not taught the truth about what happened, the hurt, I thought myself according to the influences of the world, which is the enemy of God. When we, as humans, don't know the whole story, don't have all the details, we will fill in the gaps based on our experience, feelings, and knowledge and convince ourselves it's the truth, that no one can tell you otherwise. Being a young child, I had nowhere to draw from. So I created conclusions, which are the same as judgments, influenced by ungodliness. I started judging from there. I acted on my thoughts as if truth. The formula for failure: ungodly actions plus hurt plus ungodly feelings plus ungodly thoughts equal ungodly behaviors, choices, and decisions.

I practiced and perfected this formula. I hope to deter others of you. By the age of thirty, my soul, that space or abyss in me that God created for Himself, was full of all kinds of ungodly habits and behaviors, thoughts that I created my lifestyle on.

The solution to the problem was to empty out, delete all the ungodly thoughts that had filled that space God had created for Himself. And I began filling it as my Creator had intended. That is what this book is about. And what I have been doing in collaboration with the Holy Spirit. Unbecoming everything that isn't really me, or you, so I can, and you can, be who we were meant to be in the first place. Lean not on your own understanding. I haven't always known what is right or good in the sight of God. Through revelation, I receive this knowledge, this gift I share through the reading of the Word of God, learning the ways of God, to be free of bondage.

Here is an example: My two youngest sons, at the ages of seven and eight. Father's Day was approaching, and their class was working on a project to present to their fathers.

Now, these young boys were being raised by me, a single mother. Their father was and had been in prison for the terrible crime of rape since one son was nine months old, and the younger son has never known his father outside of prison. The family kept a close relationship. The boys grew up knowing and loving their father and knew why he was in prison. However, they were so ashamed of their father's crime they refused to take part in the class project. They didn't want to tell the class or teacher anything about their father. The school contacted me because my boys had aggressive attitudes and refused to participate. I told them that their father did a bad thing but he was still their father and he loved them just like their friends' fathers did them, and that it was okay, too, for them to love their father. What their father did wrong had nothing to do with them. They had done no wrong. The shame they felt was not theirs; that was their father's shame. Their father was not all bad, for he had some good and was paying for the crime he committed. With another understanding, they were able to put that hurtful situation away in a healthy way and not fill their own souls with shame that was not theirs.

Again, serving the lust of my flesh. The old, unhealthy thinking and behavior pattern showed itself again in 2005 when my father passed and made me executor of his trust worth lots of money, on every level. Due to that circumstance, I was no longer qualified for the low-income housing program I had lived on for eleven years. But it was mine, *my* house. Like a spoiled baby, I tried to hold on to that house. I chose not to remember that I no longer was low-income, and all my children had moved out to college, so I didn't qualify for a four-bedroom house. I was once again living a lie.

Like all the other situations in my past that I had made up in my mind that I would go to any length to have what I wanted, in 2007, I convinced TH that our being married and his being incarcerated with a criminal record reflecting drug sales and possession was a violation of the Housing Authority regulations and would cause me to lose my housing if they discovered it. But if he would file for a divorce or legal separation, they couldn't, and it was free for him in there. He was all in, doing the honorable thing for his family. He said, "You know I would not let my family lose their house because of me." And it was so. We have been legally separated ever since 2008.

For the next six years, I stayed in *my* house, year after year, living the lie I created like it was true. But I was convinced that was my house. I wanted it. I fought, just short of going to jail for fraud, with all the lies I had told of my inheritance. And for years, I lied and forgot I was lying. One day, while depressed and angry, hurt and disappointed by the loss of my efforts and the fact that I had to move, that still familiar voice spoke and said, "You are wrong. You created a lie. You don't qualify for this house. It is a low-income house. God has blessed you, but you kept the lie, cheating and scheming. Stop. Repent. Thank God you are not going to jail or paying back the money for the years you have lived this lie."

Now going back to LA, where I have two houses paid for. I still didn't want to leave Yucaipa. I moved in with my daughter, her two kids, and my eldest son. That was a challenge, being displaced, living out of a box that sat in her room. Like that box, I felt in the way and unwanted. This put a real strain on the relationship. I tried to make the best out of it by showing love no matter how I felt or she treated me. Showing humility and love with the guidance, from the Holy Spirit, I was given, after living with my daughter for three months.

Back in My Egypt: The Rosebush Must Be Cut Back

I moved back to Los Angeles on December 27, 2011. I moved from Los Angeles December 30, 1988, twenty-three years to the day, almost. There is no coincidence with God. Hating it yet defeated in the fight to stay, I moved because it was the only door that made sense. I had two houses on a lot, paid for. The two-bedroom house in front, I would live in, and a one-bedroom back house I would rent out. Look at God! If you have ever lived with nothing but Jesus, you know you don't need anything but Jesus. After being back in Los Angeles with what seemed to be nothing but Jesus, I learned He is everything I need. There were many things that I wanted, but He was all that I needed. My brothers and sisters helped me out often financially. "A friend loves at all times, and a brother is born for adversity" (Prov. 17:17). I was here without a ministry, family, friend, job, and finances for the first time in twenty-three years. Yes, the liquid funds I had inherited were nearly all spent. No activities, just still and quiet all day, every day, with the Holy Spirit, in the Word, from January to April. It took months after moving in to get cable connected.

On a call from prison, TH suggested that I go back to work. I called my friend who had been a longtime friend to me over the years. As owner and CEO of her own successful faith-based residential substance abuse program, for men and woman with children, she was doing what I wanted to do. When we spoke, I told her God had moved me back to LA and I was looking for a job, and her reply was, "I have been waiting for you." She needed a director. We set a date to meet and bring in my résumé. She said she could not pay what I was worth and was used to at that time, but she would when was able. I talked about it with Stephen. He pointed out several benefits in accepting the position: opportunity to build my résumé, using my gifts and talents to build the kingdom, being productive with my time, bringing in some income. Stephen graduated with his bachelor's degree in physiology. We shared a lot of similarities and have a lot of respect and admiration for each other. One of my proudest moments as a mother was being asked to be the main speaker at the recovery program for boys my own son Stephen was director of.

I accepted the position as director I was offered. During my time there, I established great relationships with the staff, interns I trained, and many of the clients, young ladies I was given the privilege to speak life into the lives of and be an example, over a year's time. One staff member, Ms. Judy, a therapist and very influential servant for Christ, walked me through deliverance of some soul ties and generational curses made evident by my three failed marriages, which were strongholds in the way of my life, ungodly and destructive deceptions. Through that I received a new heart on May 22, 2014. Released from fear of rejection and abandonment that I had received from my father, which had plagued my relationships, causing bad habits, such as materialism, control, the need for perfection, running away, easily discarding my relationships with others. The Lord is good; His Word is truth. He speaks to His sheep, and they hear His voice. Ask and the door shall be opened. Seek and you shall find. What a treasure! I see God once again doing for me what I could not do for myself. Removing me from temporary comforts, idols, that I want to make permanent. God continues to complete the good works He started in me, saying, "Don't get comfortable. You have to keep moving. We have not reached what I have planned and purposed for you." This is God at work in my life. Everything He does is good and perfect.

He placed me at that program to serve Him. April 2012, when He brought me back to LA, twenty-four years had passed. Being shaped and formed in preparation to being used for kingdom service. I worked there three years to grow spiritually, comforting others with the same comfort I was comforted with, and to decrease my flesh (2 Cor. 1:4). When I started there, it had been more than seventeen years since a female had graduated and completed the program. In my time there as director, 90 percent stayed beyond their program completion as sober living clients. I have learned to love with true love, and that is why I believe they stayed. The call of undersubmission. No matter what, I gave my all as a servant of Christ. I love the Lord and His people. He has allowed me to lead others to the light, Jesus Christ.

TH got out of prison and came home in February 2012 to what his brother describes as a palace with everything he would want. He had great intentions to live right, starting a new life, but he was in a constant stupor. My husband was diagnosed with valley fever while in prison. The treatment for valley fever is mass doses of hard drugs. We discovered after he had been released that he had become addicted to opiates, morphine, to the drugs he had taken to treat his illness. I wish I could tell you he was in such pain that he needed the meds. But he said he felt no pain in his back. He never missed a dose, according to their prescription. He was taking pain medication in higher doses, even lethal amounts, three times per day. However, the medicine for the fungus, that one he didn't take. That one, he didn't like how it made him feel. He fought the reality of being addicted and was in a constant stupor for about sixty days. But living with myself, a controlling, mature woman and a registered addiction specialist, director of a drug rehab program with twenty-five years in recovery and passion for transformation, he made the decision to withdraw from the morphine. Without communicating what he was doing, he started on Wednesday to see if he was really addicted. I saw his discomfort, but nothing was said. And he got worse. Saturday, he got really sick in every way, and Sunday, like nothing I have ever imagined, his withdrawing was hard. He got better from that point. I have seen it in movies and read about withdrawing. I did all I knew to do to support him. Although integrity was a goal while he was in prison, the enemy was still at work. His lying and compromising took over. In April 2015, he was looking at prison time again. I wanted to be done, but I didn't want what I wanted anymore. I wanted it to be different so badly this time. I wanted to be pleasing to God, to give Him glory. Moreover, I didn't know how that could happen without Him doing it. I prayed for a miracle. I wanted us to work so bad, but it didn't happen. This idol had to go, if his need for habits came before the marriage. I couldn't believe I had married him, and now I wouldn't live with him. He chose the world, other people, places, and things. I followed the counsel of our pastor and asked him to leave the house and changed the locks. "As for me and my house, we will serve the Lord" (Josh. 24:15). We loved each other, but not enough to say no to what we each wanted. We tried to come back, but too much pride blocked the path. I was sure I was right, and he said he was right, and God would make it clear who was wrong. The Lord corrects those He loves (Prov. 3:11–12; Heb. 12:6).

The Farmer Directs
the Way You Grow

Today is Tuesday, the twelfth of June 2015, and I am now serving Jesus 24/7. Last week, Sunday, was Mother's Day. The message at church was about Joseph in the book of Genesis. During the sermon, Pastor Erwin Guevara from New Dawn Christian Village said to the congregation, "The Lord has given me a word. There is someone here that is one obedience away from your breakthrough." I knew that was a word to me. I was ready to stop walking in condemnation regarding writing this book, my testimony. Because that meant I was still walking like the world, disobedient to the Spirit (Rom. 12:1), being convicted by the Spirit repeatedly for years because of my disobedience. I had recently received a beautiful, personally engraved pen from a dear friend and woman of faith, Ms. Judy, my spiritual therapist, gave to me for my twenty-six years of transformation/recovery birthday from drugs on January 31. I received a beautiful, bound book of blank pages from my wonderful, thoughtful daughter on Mother's Day. Now I will put pen to paper and let nothing stop me. With hindsight, this is perfect timing. I have already been slow to obey for more years than I care to remember. Which is totally being disobedient.

On Friday the following week, May 22, 2015, my favorite day of the week, at the end of a very productive day at work, just before noon, my boss and longtime close friend of the family for more than thirty years, CEO and founder of the program where I worked, came into my office, asked to speak with me alone, closed the door, and said, "Ms. Sheron, today will be your last day. You have been terminated. For not providing an up-to-date certification as a registered addiction specialist." She handed me a letter of termination and two payroll checks. I told her that was not so; I went on to explain to her that my certification had been updated and completed. And I explained that I had upgraded my certi-fication to clinical supervisor. She stopped me while I was speaking and said it was not true. I could see her mind was made up. At that time, I informed her that I had never been terminated. "What do I do now?" Her response was, "Take as much time as you need to pack, but be out by the end of the day."

Trying to process what had happened, feeling unappre-ciated and uncared for, thinking how cold and unfair and unjust she had been to me, but still thinking of my clients, the ladies who had been entrusted to my care, who trusted in me as a means of assisting them in receiving treatment for their lifelong hurts and pain from relationships and aban-donment, shame, fear, and guilt that led them to substance abuse and other unhealthy, self-destructive behavior patterns. They should have been given time to detach and process the change. But now they only get three hours. I trust God. We were all His. He is in charge and will take over when you choose to give it to Him. That was what I communicated to the ladies as I spoke to them all together in the group room. That was the solution for me as well as for others. I was reminded that one reaps what he sows. In this case, I sowed only good seed, so I will reap good fruit (Gal. 6:7).

God will sort out the weeds (Matt. 13:29–30). I know what the enemy intends for harm, God will use it for my good (Gen. 50:20). His Word is true, and all things work for the good for those who are called for His purpose (Rom. 8:28). This reminds me of David when King Saul was trying to kill him. As wrong as King Saul was, David respected God's anointed and would not do anything to harm him (1 Sam. 26:3–11). God is judge. I must protect my heart and attitude so that I can hear the voice of God and obey. But my God has said to me, with desire I am to find Him on the daily path He has prepared for me. See the treasures He has placed along the path. Some are trials designed to shake me free from the world's shackles; other treasures are blessings that reveal His Presence. God said, "Search for deep treasures as you go through your day. Find Me along the way." My son Stephen, who hurts when I hurt and loves like I love, reached out to friends for prayer for his mom, and immediately 125 people responded.

A new perception. I believe that I was terminated from that job through the prompting of the Holy Spirit for such a time as this. To get my attention like only my Father knows how. I was removed from Yucaipa and all that I was busy doing, in my comfort zone, to write this testimony. But instead of listening for the Spirit guiding me to the Lord's best for me, I complained and recreated what I call good, my comfort zone, my business. Operating spiritually on autopilot, without close or constant prayer, like, "This is so familiar. I got this, Lord. I will call if I need You." My Father God loves me (Prov. 3:12). He has a plan for my life (Jer. 29:11). He has poured much into my life for His glory (Luke 12:48). A new perception about getting fired from my job so I can grow, let go, not be confused. I want to receive God's perspective on every situation I go through. I've learned that trials are opportunities, gifts from my loving heavenly Father to transform me and make me like Him.

New feelings. I appreciate her, for what she did give to my life was what I chose to do. A place to serve God, a place to belong and connect with people upon my return to Los Angeles. I needed a job and income. There were others there to meet my needs with gifts and purpose. I will stay mindful of the expectations I put on others.

Heavenly Father, thank You for Your plan to set the captives free. Thank You for wisdom and understanding that is beautiful like a rose in the midst of the thorns. Trials bring forth beauty. The thoughts come to mind are temporary, which God will burn off, remove things that were only meant to be temporary, like the flesh, the things of this world. But those things that matter are permanent. The Spirit and the fruit of the Spirit, a clean heart and a right perspective and attitude. God is at work continuously. I have negative habitual thinking errors. Like forgetting when I told God, "I hear what You are saying, Lord, about this man. That I am backsliding, relapsing, and putting him and my flesh before You, Lord. Taking risks, making ungodly choices." But I want this confronted again with the immature mentality that does not care about anything except "I want." I had established an "I want" pattern. I did not consider consequences; I only knew "I want it now." Displaying my character defects as the king baby.

And looking back at the events surrounding the end of my marriage, trying to find significance: What was this? How did I get here? I believe all things work to the good for those who love the Lord and are called according to His purpose. But so far, I cannot see a heavenly purpose. I thought I had led him to Christ and he would change his life. I believed, as he told me God told him, that I was a servant for Christ with so much love for others, but there was no one in place for loving me, and overjoyed that he had finally found his purpose in loving me. But now we know that is not it.

I need to tell you about repeating things in my life. Being back in Los Angeles, I had been thinking about divorcing TH, which led to my thinking about Social Security, since he was receiving disability, and then about Little Daddy, since he was six years older than me and we were married legally more than twenty years. So I went to the Hall of Records, Downtown LA, to get the final divorce papers, in preparation to file for one of their Social Securities, only to be told there was no new final records. I and Little Daddy were still legally married after twenty-six years. How did this happen? What do I do? I know this seems to simplify things. TH and I were never legally married—no need for the legal separation. But for me in my heart, it is more complicated, because I wanted it. I believed God for it. I hoped God would agree with my plan, see it my way. Maturity has taught me that I was the problem. When repeated things happen, it's because I haven't taken responsibility for it. Because when I am the cause and not the victim of what happens, then I can change a thing, but not until I do something different. Nothing changes and I remain a victim.

In seeking God for understanding to tell me what the truth is about TH and the problems with our marriage, I received this understanding. Running away from God is disobedience when God tells me to do something and I don't or He tells me not to do something and I do. I am running away from God, choosing to lord over my own life. A repeated pattern. And that was what I did again in 2005 when I told God, "Lord, I hear You saying, 'Don't sow to your flesh, you will

SHERON CHAMBERS JEFFERSON

reap corruption.' I moved forward in spite of Your warning because I, I, and I wanted to please my flesh." God's Word is true, and that is the problem with our so-called marriage.

Have you ever had an eye-opening moment when you were listening to someone else's story and see yourself picking the splinter out of someone's eye while you have a log hanging out of yours? (Matt. 7:3). I had an unsaved client, a practicing homosexual. She was telling me she knows it is wrong according to the Bible, God's Word, and that she believes *but* she doesn't want to stop, although these choices keep her from surrendering her life to God and causes the consequences of depression, loss of jobs/relationships, having life that has no joy, no peace. Nothing is enough. I found that I'm just like her with my choices with men. My choice in trying to find fulfillment and security within myself instead of the Lord Jesus makes them my idols. I put my desire for them over God, and when they act right according to me and my needs and worship me and do as I say, then I am fulfilled and secure, feeling like I am loved and capable of reciprocating love. But that is never enough; it doesn't last, and I am left with the truth: I have not wholeheartedly surrendered all to God. That shows a hard heart toward God. There is no difference between the two of us, she and I. Except I am willing to stop and acknowledge my sin, ask for forgiveness, all while allowing God, the strength of my life, to have His way with me. My desire is to please Him, and as He revealed the truth about me to me, I must confess and stop and repent, turn away from pleasing flesh and toward pleasing the Spirit of God (1 John 1:9; Acts 3:19).

Living a life worth living. A life with meaning. I find joy and life in the beauty of a rose. It is a work of art. Since I have been in Christ, walking with Jesus, He has made my life worth living. He is the beauty and joy of my life. He is my motivation and way and perfection of life. Life started for me when He met with me in my darkest moment and asked me to give Him my life and I said yes. That was my last dark moment, because since then, January 13, 1988, I have not had any. Just the other day, while I was cleaning the kitchen, I thought to myself about the changes that have come into my life. The thought I had was, I wonder if my father number 2, ST, knew, when he left me this inheritance, the difference it would make in my life. That I would be in the long list of those never feeling like their life has accomplished and gained worth. Inadequate. But I am now on the short list of people that own property that's paid for, secure. No longer the renter but the owner. Did he know I would never again prostitute myself for need of a man to support me? And the quiet voice of the Spirit said, "He didn't, but I did." The Spirit went on to say, "I also knew that you feel loved when you are given roses, and I put the rosebush out front, outside of your window, so every day, as you look and see a rose, you will be reminded of how much I love you, and you will never have to count on man."

All I can do is praise and worship the Lord for His love! His promise stands to never leave me, and He is the light of the World. So in the midst of all and any trial or tribulation, I have joy where there used to be sorrow. I have hope where there used to be despair. I have a future where feelings of guilt and shame and self-hate overwhelmed me. Making Jesus Lord and priority of my life, I was changed, and my life changed. Let Jesus Christ be your Source of Life, and you will start to live life like never before. I let go of my way of thinking and follow His way, by way of a new, changed perception. Jesus told them, "I am The Way, The Truth, and The Life" (John 14:6). Thorns on the Rose—a beautiful Life worth living, ever growing through your seasons of life, better and better, more and more, into what the Perfect Father and Winedresser created and purposed you to be. The beauty of the rose starts with the thorns. The hard, dark, hurtful, uncomfortable times you overcome.

The Lord is limitless. He has not given up on me, in spite of my weakness, and I am trusting Him to complete what He started in me.

Testaments

What an amazing God we serve. He loves us so much that He sent His only Son to die for our sins.

God's Word is a promise to us. Moreover, it provides us with the ability to tap into His infinite wisdom and insight.

How does one go from thinking the world revolves around them to recognizing that they are a part of the world? That's my sister, Shimmy.

As a little girl, she was smart, independent, resourceful, and, of course, manipulative. Sheron was the youngest of six children, and to call her spoiled is an understatement. We called her the joy of my mother and her father because she always got her way.

At three years old, Sheron would open the refrigerator door and prepare her own bottle. Although my mother tried to protect Sheron from the grips of the world, being as precious and curious as she is, Sheron had to experience life for herself.

Strong and resilient, as life got harder, Sheron grew tougher and her faith in the Lord became stronger. From the death of her husband to losing a child, Sheron has always remained steadfast in her faith, providing a living testimony to all. Sheron has always been unstoppable, and not because she has not faced trials and tribulations but because despite

SHERON CHAMBERS JEFFERSON

her situation, Sheron always remains the same—a proud believer and minister of God's Word.

An overcomer, a living testimony, a friend, a sister, and a confidant, my sister was born to share the gospel of the Lord. Her joy through the rain spirit has been a driving force and her strongest virtue since I can remember. Her infectious spirit and in-your-face attitude are gifts from God—one that we can all be grateful for. Romans 10:15 says, "How will they preach unless they are sent?" Just as it is written, "How beautiful are the feet of those who bring good news of good things?"

Shimmy, your steps have been perfectly ordained and carefully planted before you were born. I love you and can't hardly wait to dance with you and Nana in heaven.

Love,
Your big sister, Renee Walker

Who loves me more and who do I love the *moistest?* My big sister. It's truly amazing how God works all things together for the good of us that love Him, that includes people and relationships. You see, my big sister, who at one point was grooming me to be a gigolo/drug dealer, is now my closest confidant in Christ. She has demonstrated before me what it means to be brought back from dark places, even when you're the one who took yourself there.

Thank you, Sheron. You've shared with me your most difficult trials and been with me through mine. Our mama was both your best friend and mine. I thank God that when she left us for glory, she left us with each other. I know I don't have to say it, but I will—I love you so much.

From the new baby that took your crib,
Your big head little brother, Shelly Fisher III

They say it takes a village to raise a child. I had a village of uncles and aunts. Most of them were grown and busy starting their own families as I was growing up. I was the baby in the house, and the rule was "don't hit the baby."

One of my aunts made sure that the rule was enforced. She became my protector at a young age. Her name is Sheron Ann. I always called her Shern. Shern would always make sure no one hit the baby (me). She continued to be my protector even as I got older.

In my late teens, my home life became troubled. By this time, she was a single parent struggling with her own kids. She had an open door policy for me and again protected me and took care of me. It didn't matter that she had babies depending on her financially. She took me in, put a roof over my head, and fed me. I'm sure it was a struggle to have to feed another person, but she *never* complained. She always made sure that I was okay. I've been blessed to have her as part of my village, and I'm grateful to God for putting her in my life.

Tracy Gentry

What a dynamic woman of God! Battle-tested and proven! Many times, when we think of the word *endurance* being personified in characters of literature and history, we rarely have the chance of seeing those examples in real-life, personal relationships. I can say that I have been blessed to see this walking, living testament of Christ Jesus in my lifetime! She has been an example of a purpose-driven life, a rock to her family, and a true soldier in the army.

I am so blessed to see you accomplish this great feat and inspired to continually seek the higher calling because of what I have witnessed God does in and through your life! Your presence in this world gives me great hope in murky times. Because you are here, I know souls will be encouraged. Because you are here, I know that lives will be enhanced.

I have been such a recipient of your love. I stopped calling you my "stepmom" years ago in my teens and dubbed you the title "Mama Sheron." I am a man of forty-five years now, and I am amazed that I have never seen you stop growing! I have not seen you grow old in your soul or bitter. You are a *blessing* to every relationship you purpose to pour into! Continue your course…continue the marathon!

With great respect and love,
Robert Colvin

Sheron is my husband's little (big) sister. From the first time I met her, I felt a strong connection. Her heart is so open to receive and give love. This part of her did not waver during her time of addiction. We did not see much of her during this time, but she always stayed in touch with us.

The day I remember the most is the third of July in 1983. We drove her out to Ontario Community Hospital where she admitted herself in for rehab. It was a quiet ride out there. I'm sure she was nervous, and we were hopeful. One the way back home, we watched the beautiful fireworks and prayed for her recovery. July 4, what a perfect day for her to admit herself into rehab. This will be the start of her independence.

After this, she had a few slips, but she moved out of LA and brought the Lord into her life. Moving out of LA gratefully was the best thing she ever did. Of course, accepting the Lord as her Savior was definitely the thing that truly saved her. And from which I know, moving out of LA was good for her, but I truly missed her close to us.

After all four of the kids grew up and moved out, she came back to LA. So I now have my sister, my friend, back close, and it has been so great. But I know she wants to move back to Yucaipa or Beaumont, where her children and grandchildren are living. And I pray that she will be able to move up there with them. And again, I will miss her, but wherever she moves to, I love my sister, my friend.

Janice Harper

Sheron—that word means rose. What does that mean? It means that though beautiful, you cannot get too close or you can be pricked.

This describes my friend, my girl, my sister in Christ. I met her back in 1991, six months after arriving in a bold new world of America. You see, I was not born here, just came for school. I got a scholarship to attend college. Through a lot of misfortunes, I met my friend. Of course, we were not friends from the beginning.

She was troubled on every side yet not distressed (2 Cor. 4:8a). However, she had her days. Arguing over a burnt pan, not realizing that God was burning away all the gunk from her life. We took a lot of long walks to be healthy and to lose weight, but it was the walking in the Spirit (Gal. 5:16) that we needed to accomplish. She taught me true forgiveness and what that looks like, yet it was that same forgiveness that was extremely hard for her to accomplish in herself. She finally became aware of the fact that where the Spirit of the Lord is, there is liberty (2 Cor. 3:17b).

Her growth began when she realized that God has commanded the light to shine out of darkness in her heart to give the light of knowledge of the glory of God in the face of Jesus Christ (2 Cor. 4:6). She began to see God for who He truly is—her *everything*! She began to realize that nothing she does apart from Him will prosper. Nothing she thinks about or try to do apart from *Him* will manifest. As 2 Corinthians 3:5 states, "Not that we are sufficient of ourselves to think anything as of ourselves; but our sufficiency is of God."

SHERON CHAMBERS JEFFERSON

Now she can truly sing the song of 2 Corinthians 4:7–10:

> But I have this treasure in my earthen vessel, that the excellency of the power may be of God and not of me. I am troubled on every side, yet not distressed; I am perplexed, but not in despair; persecuted, but not forsaken, cast down, but not destroyed. Always bearing about in my body the dying of the Lord Jesus, that the life also of Jesus might be made manifest in my body.

My friend took a journey. This journey took her through disappointments, heartaches, sadness, unforgiveness, bitterness, loneliness, and things uncomfortable, but she needed to go through these things. As she went through experiencing each situation, God was able to break something else off and mold her back into what *He* wanted. Now she is rooted and grounded in *Him*. There can be no turning back.

I heard it said that there is a reason why the mirror looking back is smaller than the one looking forward. You can reflect on what is past but only to see how far you have come. I saw her at the beginning, and I see her now. The transformation is phenomenal, but God only do phenomenal.

Sharon Vassell-High

Where do I begin? My mother is an extraordinary woman. Although she has been a mother to many, I am her only biological daughter. Out of the six children she's brought into this world, the Lord gave her only one daughter. We have always had a special relationship. I've been her right hand since I can remember, helping her take care of my brothers and the household. She's taught me to be the responsible, independent, hardworking, and caring woman that I am. Watching her lead by example, she has instilled integrity, self-esteem, and godly characteristics within me. My mother has faults, as we all do, but she is one of the most loving and genuine beings on this earth. My whole life, she's taken in people off the streets, who had no place to go, and provided a safe, loving, and comfortable home. I take pride in being her daughter and watching others love and respect her because of who she is.

I love you, Momma!
Shannon Colvin

What do you say about a woman who saved your life? Before meeting Sheron, I wouldn't step foot into a church, let alone talk to anyone about God. I was sixteen years old and at the lowest part of my adolescent life when God brought Sheron into my life and saved me in every aspect a human being could. It's because of you, Sheron, that I have a life to be proud of, a God who I now call father, and a strong foundation to withstand any storm all because of the life tools you have given me thirteen years ago. If there is a testament of God's love, compassion, faithfulness, and glory, it would be Sheron. Thank you for the continued love and support you have given me over the years and years to come. I am honored to not only be a part of your life but to have the honor of calling you Mom.

Brittany Dean

I spent eighteen years of my life marching along the path of misery and darkness when I first met Ms. Sheron Chambers. It had been a month since I received Jesus Christ as my Lord and Savior at the Set Free Church Men's Discipleship Ranch, and yet I still wasn't sure of who I was or where I was going. I held on dearly to the world's cure of sobriety though I never seemed to understand how I could keep it when all I ever did was fail at it multiple times before in my life. Sheron was teaching a drug and alcohol class at Set Free Church that I had to attend due to a court sentence. It was there at these classes that Sheron would show me, through her relationship with Jesus, who Jesus was and who He truly created me to be.

Sheron is gifted by the Holy Spirit in exhortation and teaching, and with these gifts, I was poured into with great compassion that only one whom knew the Lord could offer. She understood the struggles of someone who knew only what the world taught them to be and what they heard they would never become. Sheron loves the Lord, and in turn, she loves those who He puts in her path. Through the Spirit of God, she helped me pull the world's ideas from my heart and mind while pointing me to Jesus in filling them back up with truth. I was shown that addiction wasn't my problem; the sin and the desire to fill an empty place in my heart meant for only God to fill was the problem. Sheron showed me that Jesus did live within me and that I wasn't a drug addict meant for failure but instead I am a beloved child of God with incredible power given by the Spirit of Christ. She showed me the truth about who I am in Christ and what I truly needed to overcome all the obstacles in life that most people never expected me to get around. With her encour-

SHERON CHAMBERS JEFFERSON

agement and inspired spiritual insights, I was able to not just go around these obstacles, but I was also brought through them in Christ Jesus.

Thank you, Ms. Sheron, for your support, encouragement, compassion, love, and for delivering God's truth. To those who will read this book, I would implore you to take hold of the many lessons of this experiential knowledge of who Jesus is and what He can do. The knowledge that Ms. Sheron has shared through her words in order to fuel the desires of our hearts to know Him intimately, a love that goes beyond our minds and into our hearts.

God bless,
Pastor Josh

So when I think of Sheron, I think of the story of when an angel of the Lord appeared to Gideon. He said, "God is with you, mighty warrior." She's been a mother to me; she's also been a friend and confidant. I wanted to cling to her, but she wouldn't let me. She continues to point me to Jesus to this very day. I am so grateful for the woman of God that she is. She impacted my life and has played a huge role in my adventure in Christ.

Love,
Jasmaine Taylor

When I was at the lowest point in my life, it was God who was there to carry me through to the other side. He put in my life a counselor, mentor, teacher, family member, and friend in the form of Ms. Sheron Chambers-Jefferson. A true blessing to me. You see, I had abused drugs for the past eleven years, was homeless, hopeless, and helpless. I came to the rehabilitation center only seeking safe shelter because I was just so extremely exhausted from living on the streets. It never even occurred to me that I needed to change my life or even to consider stopping the use of drugs.

I did not know it then but that all changed on the day when I met Ms. Sheron. She welcomed me in her over-whelming, capable, loving arms and let me know that I was safe. She listened to me as I told her my entire life story, a long downward spiral that led me ultimately to that moment in time. She did not judge me but let me know we had a lot of serious work to do and that the first thing I needed to do was speak to God… It was up to me too, but I was not alone. She had my back, and I had nothing to fear.

When I did speak to God, I found out that God still loves me and that I could change my behaviors, ask for forgiveness, repent my sins, and change my life. Ms. Sheron was there supporting me all the way with her Bible study class and her one-on-one sessions as well. No matter how crazy the things I told her were, she never judged me. Yet when I would break her rules, sometimes on purpose even, she would be right there to administer strong discipline on me. This discipline usually came in the form of writing out Bible lessons or sometimes cleaning chores too.

One life-changing Bible lesson that Ms. Sheron taught me was "delayed gratification"—the principle of not having everything you want immediately. She taught me this by having me look up the Bible scriptures that supported this idea. She then had me write in my own words what it meant to me and how I could apply it to my life. Perhaps twenty pages later, she discussed the topic with me in her office to make sure I truly understood why she had chosen the topic for me specifically. I have never forgotten this lesson because it has been very valuable to me. I still use it when I make decisions about what I want now or what can really wait. It taught me patience in all things basically.

That is just a one small example of the many things that I learned from Ms. Sheron. I would say the most important lesson I learned was how to have a closer relationship with God and with myself. She showed me that I am not a waste, that God has a plan for my life, that even I am worthy of love. She showed me how to stop using drugs, how to live sober, and how to have self-respect—all these things I had given up on previously or simply forgot how to do. The best way to describe it is that Ms. Sheron was a light bulb in a dark room. She guided me out of the hole I had made for myself, gave me hope, and guided the way.

I am so excited to see what else Ms. Sheron has in store for all of us, how many more people she will lead to God, how many more she can help, and how many more she will touch. My life is forever better from the time I was blessed to spend in her loving care. I pray that others will get to experience her generosity the way I have. God bless you, Ms. Sheron, and thank you.

Yours truly,
Nicole Anderson

Ms. Sheron has been one of the most influential people in my life. Working with her was definitely a breath of fresh air for me. She gave the most helpful advice and suggestions and was always ready to shower you with love, strength, wisdom, and courage. I will always love this lady because she has constantly shown me that no matter what race, gender, age, or preference of life, she is always there to listen to you, laugh with you, and love on you with everything she has without judgment!

I love you, Ms. Sheron!
Precious

CPSIA information can be obtained
at www.ICGtesting.com
Printed in the USA
LVHW031941250521
688446LV00005B/87